Dedication

*"I would like to dedicate this program to all those
who ever struggled with learning a foreign language
and to Wolfgang Karfunkel"*

Also by Yatir Nitzany

Conversational French Quick and Easy

....

Conversational Portuguese Quick and Easy

....

Conversational Spanish Quick and Easy

....

Conversational Italian Quick and Easy

....

Conversational Russian Quick and Easy

....

Conversational German Quick and Easy

....

Conversational Hebrew Quick and Easy

....

Conversational Yiddish Quick and Easy

....

Conversational Arabic Quick and Easy
(Lebanese Dialect)

Conversational Language Quick *and* Easy

A GUIDE TO THE MOST COMMONLY USED WORDS OF EVERY LANGUAGE

YATIR NITZANY

FORWARD

ABOUT MYSELF

For many years I struggled to learn Spanish, and still knew no more than about 20 words and consequently was extremely frustrated. One day I stumbled upon this method as I was playing around with word combinations. Suddenly I came to the realization that every language has a certain core group of words that are most commonly used in a language, and simply by learning them, one could gain ability to engage in fluent communication..

I discovered which those words were, narrowed them down to 350, and that once memorized, one could then connect and create one's own sentences. THE VARIATIONS WERE and ARE, INFINITE!!! By using this incredibly simple technique I could converse at a proficient level and speak Spanish. Within a week I astonished my Spanish speaking friends with my new found ability. The following semester I registered at my university for a Spanish Speaking Course and I applied the same principles I learned in that class (grammar, additional vocabulary, future and past tense, etc.) to those 350 words I already had memorized **and immediately I felt as if I had grown wings and learned how to fly.** At the end of the semester we took a class trip to San José, Costa Rica. I was like a fish in water, while the rest of my classmates were floundering and still struggling to converse.

Throughout the following months I again applied the same principle to other languages, French, Portuguese, Italian, and Arabic all of which I now speak proficiently thanks to this very simple technique. This method is by far the fastest way to master fluent conversation. There is no other technique that compares to my concept. It is effective, it worked for me and it will work for you. Be consistent with my program and you too will succeed the way I and many, many others have.

Table of Contents

Introduction

People often dream about learning a foreign language, but never do. Whatever the reason is, it's time to set it aside. With my new method, you will have enough time and you will not fail. You will actually learn how to speak the fundamentals of any language in this book, and speak the language fluently in as little as four days. You won't speak Shakespeare at first, but you will gain significant proficiency in any language you choose. For example, visiting the country of the language you will study, you will almost effortlessly engage in basic "fluent" communication with its locals. No longer will you be intimidated with culture shock. It's time to relax. Learning a language is a valuable skill and a form of communication that connects people of multiple cultures around the world.

How does my method work? Well, I have taken twenty-seven of the most used languages and distilled out of them the most commonly used words in any sentence. This whole process took three years of observation and research. In that time, I have also picked these words out in such a way that they are structurally interrelated and when combined form sentences. In fact, there are only nine basic words that will effectively build bridges, enabling you to speak in an understandable manner. The words will also correspond easily in sentences to ask someone how their meal was last night or ask directions.

My book is intended for basic vocal communication, meaning, anyone can easily use it to "get by" linguistically while visiting a country, without learning the entire language. Though you will be speaking mostly in the infinitive tense, you will be 100 percent understandable to native speakers. **One disclaimer: this is not a grammar book, though it does address minute and essential grammar rules.** Still, this is only the basics. Therefore, understanding complex sentences with obscure words in a language are outside the scope of this book.

I have spent several years determining which words I felt were most important for this method of basic "fluent" communication. Most people who have tried this method have also been successful. Grouped by continental region, these twenty-seven languages are translated into Latin letters, so it is not a requirement to know the written form of the foreign language beforehand. By the time you finish my book, you will be 90 percent fluent and understandable in any language you choose. This is the best basis to learn a language, and it has never been done before. (Please also see the "Note to the Reader" on page #205 of this book).

This book will serve as your guide to the 350 most commonly used words in every language. Whenever you are ready to become conversational in any of these 27 languages, just open this book and have a go at it!

Directions

The following 5 pages are a comprehensive list of the 350 most used words in every language. You will encounter these 5 charts for each of the 27 languages in this book. The first page consists of the pronouns. The second and third pages consist of the adjectives, adverbs, prepositions, conjunctions, interjections, and nouns. Fourth page are the most commonly used verbs. The fifth page, Building Bridges, will teach you how to link the verbs, in the conjugated and infinitive forms, as well as 2-3 sample sentences and some additional minute grammar rules; again this is NOT a grammar book!!

Part 1: The Prounouns

I
Me
My
Mine
His
Him
Her
Hers
He
She
Us
Our
With you
With You {Plural}
With her
With him
With Them
Without me
Without
Without you
Without you {Plural}
Them, They
Their
You
You {Plural}
I am
I was
I will
Are you
We
Without her
Without Them
Without Him
With me
For you
To be
Yours
We are
With us
Without us
Who

Part 2: Adjectives, adverbs, prepositions, conjunctions, interjections

What	Something
If	Sometimes
Similar	Somewhere
Where	Yes
Were	No
When	Less
Only	Instead
Was	Including
Other	While
Since	Someone
Same	Again
With	Away
Already	But
Together	Don't
Then	Both
Than	Because
More	Still, Yet
Very	Time *(how many times)*
Much, a lot	Time *(era)*
From	Time *(hour)*
And	Also, too, as well
Before	Around
After	Never
Afterwards	Of Course
To	Here
The	This
That *(demonstrative pronoun)*	OK
That *(conjunction)*	Just
Is	Although
Which	Through
For	It is
Of	Everywhere
Against	Ready
Always	Soon
Until	Except
Everything	Between
Every	Now
Even If	Later
Things	Toward
There	How Much & How Many
Into	Neither
Or	None
On	Nobody
About	Maybe
How	Way
In	Why
Nothing	Side
At	Everybody
Almost	A Few

In this program there are certain words which sound the same, spelled the same, and are pronounced the same however they have different meanings. Such as *time* and *that*. So keep your eyes peeled.

Part 3: Additional adjectives, adverbs, prepositions, conjunctions, interjections, nouns, and a few of the most common phrases.

Small	Name
Big	Last name
Hot	What is your name
Cold	How old are you
Up	Welcome
Down	Years
Person	Sky
People	Night
Fast	Light
Slow	Darkness
Day	Morning
Tomorrow	House
Today	Car
Yesterday	Left
Good	Right
Bad	Place
Hello	Straight
Goodbye	Parents
How are you	Book
Nice to meet you	Problem
Good Night	Behind
Good Afternoon	Front
Good Morning	Near
Friend	Far
Mom	Sun
Dad	Better
Brother	Worse
Sister	Beautiful
Cousin	Real
Grandfather	Easy
Grandmother	Hard
Please	Next
Thank you	One
Sorry	Two
New	Three
Inside	Four
Outside	Five
Different	Six
First	Seven
Last	Eight
Child	Nine
Man	Ten
Women	Number
Week	Month

Part 4: The verbs

To Talk	To Drive
To Walk	To Pay
To Run	To Buy
To Sleep	To Practice
To Begin	To Prepare
To Finish	To Meet
To Drink	To Fly
To Smoke	To Visit
To Prefer	To Swim
To Loose	To Show
To Forget	To Know
To Hold	To Think
To Follow	To Believe
To Continue	To Love
To Want	To Like
To Stay	To Use
To Keep	To Try
To Play	To Understand
To Get	To Have
To Help	To Happen
To Go	To Recognize
To Give	To Hear
To Receive	To Listen
To Bring	To Press
To Work	To Promise
To Hope	To Choose
To Live	To Arrive
To Find	To Leave *(to leave a place)*
To Look	To Leave *(to leave an object)*
To Search	To Do
To See	To Order
To Read	To Pretend
To Write	To Change
To Learn	I Can
To Teach	To Return
To Take	To Borrow
To Turn on	To Sit
To Turn off	To Need
To Close	To Say
To Put	To Remove
To Allow	To Travel
To Lift	To Eat
To Open	To Exchange
To Wish	To Mix
To Enter	To Belong
To Come	To Feel
To Move	To Stop
To Rent	To Ask
To Remember	To Answer
To Check	To Decide
To Call	To Sell
To Resemble	To Wait

Here we have the verb *to leave*, which has two different meaning, so keep your eyes peeled when encountering it in the program.

Part 5: Building Bridges and other Grammatical Exercises

This section is referred to as "Building bridges and other grammatical exercises" and may be one of the most useful of the five pages. In this page we take what we have already learned and apply it all together and we build bridges. The way building bridges works is, these nine conjugated words, which have been selected after studies I have conducted for several months to determine which words are most commonly conjugated into first person and which are then automatically followed by an infinitive verb. For example once you know how to say, "I Go", "I Like", "I Need", "I Want" it will enable you to say almost anything you want more proper and understandable. Please note the word "I Can" is also followed by an infinitive verb in most other languages, but not in English, so make sure you focus on that word when learning the language of your desire from this book.

I Can
I Do
I Go
I Like
I Need
I Say
I See
I Talk
I Want

I go to the house without you
I like to live in Miami now
I need to find the place to visit
I want to see you at my house tomorrow

Tip to the Reader:

Once the memorization of the 350 words, of the language of your desire, has been attained then there is no doubt that you will be able to combine words and speak fluently. But if it's done prior, or while, attending a class in that language, it will be extremely beneficial because then you could add everything you learned in that class (grammar, sentence structure, past and future tense, etc.) on top of those 350 words, which you have just mastered, AND you will be amazed!!

Language learning classes aren't as effective, in providing you the ability to engage in fluent communications, as much as this program will. Foreign language classes teach you everything BESIDES how to become conversational, you will be required to take at least 4-5 semesters of that language in order for you to come anywhere close to what you can achieve with my program. But if you combine the two, the class with this program, you will grow wings and learn to fly as I did!

Chapter 1: European Languages

Section I: Latin Languages
- French
- Italian
- Portuguese
- Spanish

The French Language

In the 16th century, King Francis I declared French as his nation's official language. Little did he know it was soon to become the 15th most common language in the world and the official language of 29 countries. However, the language has declined in popularity since its peak in the 16th and 17th centuries. The French language was once a symbol of prestige, that is, only the high class and educated spoke it. For example, Russia's Catherine the Great knew French, as well as Prussia's Frederick II. Although the present French language has many dialects according to the country's regions, it is still known as France's official language.

Spoken in: France, including French Overseas Departments, Communities and Territories; Canada especially in Quebec and New Brunswick; Belgium; Switzerland; Luxembourg; Monaco; Morocco; Algeria; Tunisia; many Western and Central African nations such as Ivory Coast, the Democratic Republic of the Congo, Niger and Senegal; Haiti; Mauritius;

I	Je
Me	Je
My	Mon
Mine	
His	Sien
Him	Il
Her	Elle
Hers	Sien
He	Il
She	Elle
Us	Nous
Our	Notre
Ours	Notres
With you	Avec Vous
With You {Plural}	Avec Vous
With her	Avec Elle
With him	Avec Lui
With Them	Avec Eux
Without me	Sans moi
Without	Sans
Without you	Sans Vous
Without you {Plural}	Sans Vous
Them	Ils
Their	Leur
You	Vous
You {Plural}	Vous
I am	Je Suis
I was	J'ai Ete
I will	Je ferai
Are you	Vous sont
They	Ils
Without her	Sans Elle
Without Them	Sans Eux
Without Him	Sans Lui
With me	Avec Moi
For you	Pour vous
To be	Être
Yours	Le vôtre
We are	Nous sommes
With us	Avec nous
Without us	Sans nous
Who	Qui

What	Ce Qui	**Something**	Quelque chose
If	Si	**Sometimes**	Parfois
Like {as}	Comme	**Somewhere**	Quelque part
Where	Ou	**Yes**	Oui
Were	Étaient	**No**	Non
When	Quand	**Less**	Moins
Only	Seulement	**Instead**	À la place
Was	Etait	**Including**	Incluant
Other	Autre	**While**	Pendant que
Since	Depuis	**Someone**	Quelqu'un
Same	Meme	**Again**	Encore
With	Avec	**Away**	Loin
Already	Déjà	**But**	Mais
Together	Ensemble	**Don't**	Pas
Then	Alors	**Both**	Tous les deux
Than	Que	**Because**	Puisque
More	Plus	**Still, Yet**	Toujours
Very	Très	**Time**	Fois
Much, a lot	Mucho	**Time**	Temps
From	De	**Time**	Heure
And	Et	**Also, Too**	Aussi
Before	Avant	**Around**	Autour
After	Ensuite	**Never**	Jamais
Afterwards	Après	**Of course**	Bien sûr
To	à	**Here**	Ici
The	Le {M}, La {F}	**This**	Ceci
That	Cela	**OK**	OK
That	Que	**Just**	Juste
Is	Il Est	**Although**	Quoique
Which	Lequel	**Through**	à travers
For	Del	**It is**	
Of	De	**Everywhere**	Partout
Against	Contre	**Ready**	Préparent
Always	Toujours	**Soon**	Bientôt
Until	Jusqu' à	**Except**	Excepté
Everything	Tout	**Between**	Entre
Every	Chaque	**Now**	Maintenant
Even If	Même	**Later**	plus tard
Thing	Chose	**Toward**	Vers
There	Là	**How Much & How Many**	
Close	Encelar	**Neither**	Ni l'un ni l'autre
Or	Là	**None**	Aucun
On	Sur	**Nobody**	Personne
About	Sur	**Maybe**	Peut-être
How	Comment	**Way**	Manière
In	Dans	**Why**	Pourquoi
Nothing	Rien	**Side**	Prendre parti
At	A	**Everybody**	Tout le monde
Almost	Presque	**A Few**	Quelques uns

Small	Petit	**Name**	Nom
Big	Grand	**Last name**	Nom de famille
Hot	Chaud	**What is you name**	Quel âge vous êtes
Cold	Froid	**How old are you**	Quelle age aver vous
Up	Haut	**Welcome**	Bienvenue
Down	Bas	**Years**	Année
Person	Personne	**Sky**	Ciel
People	Gens	**Night**	Nuit
Fast	Rapide	**Light**	Lumière
Slow	Lent	**Darkness**	Obscurité
Day	Jour	**Morning**	Matin
Tomorrow	Demain	**House**	Maison
Today	Aujourd'hui	**Car**	Voiture
Yesterday	Hier	**Left**	Gauche
Good	Bon	**Right**	Droite
Bad	Mauvais	**Place**	Endroit
Hello	Bonjour	**Straight**	Droit
Goodbye	Au revoir	**Parents**	Parents
How are you	Comment allez	**Book**	Livre
Nice to meet you	C'est un plaisir de vous rencontre	**Problem**	Problème
Good Night	Bonne nuit	**Behind**	Derrière
Good Afternoon	Bon après-midi	**Front**	Devant
Good Morning	Bonjour	**Near**	À cote
Friend	Ami	**Far**	Loin
Mom	Maman	**Sun**	Soleil
Dad	Papa	**Better**	Mieux
Brother	Frère	**Worse**	Pire
Sister	Soeur	**Beautiful**	Beau
Cousin	Cousin	**Real**	Vrai
Grandfather	Grand-père	**Easy**	Facile
Grandmother	Grand-mère	**Hard**	Dur
Please	Se il vous plaît	**Next**	Prochain
Thank you	Merci	**One**	Un
Sorry	Désolé	**Two**	Deux
New	Nouveau	**Three**	Trois
Inside	L'intérieur	**Four**	Quatre
Outside	En dehors de	**Five**	Cinq
Different	Différent	**Six**	Six
First	D'abord	**Seven**	Sept
Last	Bout	**Eight**	Huit
Child	Enfant	**Nine**	Neuf
Man	Homme	**Ten**	Dix
Women	Femmes	**Number**	Nombre
Week	Semaine	**Month**	Mois

To Talk	Parler	**To Drive**	Conduire
To Walk	Marcher	**To Pay**	Payer
To Run	Courir	**To Buy**	Acheter
To Sleep	Dormir	**To Practice**	Pratiquer
To Begin	Commencer	**To Prepare**	Préparer
To Finish	Finir	**To Meet**	Se réunir
To Drink	Boire	**To Fly**	Voler
To Smoke	À la Fumée	**To Visit**	Visiter
To Prefer	Préférer	**To Swim**	Nager
To Loose	Pedre	**To Show**	Montrer
To Forget	Oubiler	**To Know**	Savoir
To Hold	Se tenir	**To Think**	Penser
To Follow	Suivre	**To Believe**	Croire
To Continue	Couninuer	**To Love**	Aimer
To Want	Vouloir	**To Like**	Aimer
To Stay	Rester	**To Use**	Employer
To Keep	Garder	**To Try**	Essayer
To Play	Au jeu	**To Understand**	Comprendre
To Get	Obtenir	**To Have**	Avoir
To Help	Aider	**To Happen**	Produirer
To Go	Aller	**To Recognize**	Reconnaître
To Give	Donner	**To Hear**	Entendre
To Receive	Receive	**To Listen**	Écouter
To Bring	Apporter	**To Press**	Pression
To Work	Travailler	**To Promise**	Promettre
To Hope	Espérer	**To Choose**	Choisir
To Live	Vivre	**To Arrive**	Arriver
To Find	Vivre	**To Leave**	Partir
To Look	Trouver	**To Leave {Something}**	Laisser
To Search	Chercher pour	**To Do**	Faire
To See	Voir	**To Order**	Commande
To Read	Lire	**To Pretend**	Feindre
To Write	Écrire	**To Change**	Changer
To Learn	Apprendre	**I Can**	Je Puex
To Teach	Enseigner	**To Return**	Retourner
To Take	Prendre	**To Borrow**	Emprunter
To Turn on	Allumer	**To Sit**	Reposer
To Turn Off	Éteindre	**To Need**	Avoir besoin
To Close	Fermer	**To Say**	Dire
To Put	Mettre	**To Remove**	Sortir
To allow	Laisser	**To Travel**	Voyage
To Lift	Soulever	**To Eat**	Manger
To Open	Ouvrir	**To Exchange**	Échanger
To Wish	Souhaiter	**To Mix**	Mélanger
To Enter	Entrer	**To Belong**	Appartenir
To Come	Venir	**To Feel**	Sentir
To Move	Déplacer	**To Stop**	Arrêt
To Rent	Louer	**To Ask**	Demander
To Remember	Rappeler	**To Answer**	Répondre
To Check	Vérifier	**To Decide**	Décider
To Call	D'appeler	**To Sell**	Vendre
To Resemble	Ressembler	**To Wait**	Attendre

Building Bridges

I Can	Je Peux
I Do	Je Fais
I Go	Je Vais
I Need	J'Ai besoin de
I Want	Je Veux
I See	Je Vois
I Like	J'Aime
I Say	Je Dis
I Talk	Je Parle

Phrases:

I don't understand you
Je ne comprends vous

How do you say that in English?
Comment dit-on cela en Anglais?

Rules

If it's a question then the pronouns; you, he, I, etc... then first comes the verb and then the pronoun.
For example in English: "Do you speak French"
In French: "Parle {speak} vous {you} Frances {French}"

-First the noun and then the adjective
For example in English: Sun glasses
In French: Verres {Glasses} du {of} Soleil {Sun}

For the French language; grammar, pronunciation, accent, conjugation, reading, and sentence structure are recommended but not required for non-Shakespearean speakers.

French Pronunciation

Ch – sh
C – s {sit)
G – gzh
Gn – ni (g silent)
H – silent
Qu – k
W – usually like v sound
É – ay
È – eh
j- zh
o, ait, aî ,
ei – eh
ô – oa
eu, eû – ur
ail, aille – ie
oeu – euile,
euille – vhy
ui – wee
ou, oû – oo
am, an – ahng em, en
ien – yang im, in, aim, ain, eim,
ein – awng om, on, om,
un – ang

If a constant is at end of the word, the last letter of the
word will NOT be pronounced
For example: "to go" – "allez" pronounced "*alle*"
"I can" – "je peux" pronounced "*je puu*"

Italian

The official language of Italy, Italian started detailed and complex. It has evolved over time, primarily due to the poet Dante Alighieri, who modernized the language by blending the Italian dialects, Sicilian and Tuscan. While the language's Tuscan roots are more prevalent, the now extinct language, Dalmation, also inspired Dante. With the combination of these three Romantic dialects, the Italian language evolved into its modern state. Spoken by approximately 70 million people, Italian shares the title with Latin as co-official language of the Vatican City, as Italian closely mirrors Latin roots. Though the language is most widely spoken in Italy, Italian is also spoken in some areas of Switzerland, Croatia, France, Slovenia and Albania.

Spoken in: Italy, Malta

I	Io
Me	Me
My	Mio
Mine	La/ Il Mio/a
His	Suo
Him	Lui
Her	Lei
Hers	Il suo
He	Lui
She	Lei
Us	Noi
Our	Nostro
With you	Con te
With You {Plural}	Con voi
With her	Con lei
With him	Con lui
With Them	Con Loro
Without me	Senza me
Without	Senza
Without you	Senza te
Without you {Plural}	Senza voi
Them	Loro
Their	Loro
You	Tu
You {Plural}	
I am	Sono
I was	Ero
I will	Farò
Are you	Loro
They	Loro
Without her	Senza lei
Without Them	Senza Loro
Without Him	Senza lui
With me	Con me
For you	Per te
To be	Per essere
Yours	Tuo
We are	Siamo
With us	Con noi
Without us	Senza noi
Who	Chi

What	Che	Something	Qualcosa
If	Se	Sometimes	A volte
Similar	Simile	Somewhere	In qualche luogo
Where	Dove	Yes	Sì
Were	Erano	No	No
When	Quando	Less	Meno
Only	Soltanto	Instead	Invece
Was	Era	Including	Includere
Other	L'altro	While	Mentre
Since	Poiché	Someone	Qualcuno
Same	Come	Again	Ancora
With	Con	Away	Lontano
Already	Già	But	Ma
Together	Insieme	Don't	Non fare
Then	Poi	Both	Entrambi
Than	Di	Because	Perché
More	Più	Still, Yet	Tuttavia
Very	Molto	Time	Volta
Much, a lot	Molto	Time	Tempo
From	Da	Time	Ora
And	E	Also, Too	Anche
Before	Prima	Around	Intorno
After	Dopo	Never	Non mai
Afterwards	Successivamente	Of Course	Claro
To	A, per	Here	Qui
The	Il, la, l', gli, le	This	Questo
That	Ciò	OK	OK
That	Che	Just	Giusto
Is	É	Although	Sebbene
Which	Quale	Through	Attraverso
For	Per	It is	È
Of	Di	Everywhere	Ovunque
Against	Contro	Ready	Pronto
Always	Sempre	Soon	Presto
Until	Finché	Except	Eccetto
Everything	Tutto	Between	Tra
Every	Ogni	Now	Adesso
Even If	Anche Se	Later	Dopo
Thing{s}	Cose	Toward	Verso
There	Lí	How Much & How Many	Quanto
Into	In	Neither	Né
Or	O	None	Nessuno
On	Su	Nobody	Non nessuno
About	Circa	Maybe	Forse
How	Come	Way	La maniera
In	In	Why	Perché
Nothing	Non niente	Side	Parte
At	A	Everybody	Tutti
Almost	Quasi	A Few	Alcuni

Small	Piccolo	Name	Nome
Big	Grande	Last name	Cognome
Hot	Caldo	What is your name	Come ti chiami
Cold	Il freddo	How old are you	Quanit anni hai
Up	Su	Welcome	Benvenuto
Down	Giù	Years	Gli anni
Person	Persona	Sky	Cielo
People	Persone	Night	Notte
Fast	Veloce	Light	Luce
Slow	Rallentare	Darkness	L'oscurità
Day	Giorno	Morning	Mattina
Tomorrow	Domani	House	Casa
Today	Oggi	Car	L'automobile
Yesterday	Ieri	Left	La sinistra
Good	Buono, bene	Right	Destra
Bad	Cattivo	Place	Luogo
Hello	Ciao	Straight	Diritto
Goodbye	Arrivederci	Parents	Genitori
How are you	Come stai	Book	Libro
Nice to meet you	Piacere	Problem	Problema
Good Night	La Notte buona	Behind	Dietro
Good Afternoon	Buon Pomeriggio	Front	Davanti
Good Morning	Buon giorno	Near	Vicino
Friend	L'amico	Far	Lontano
Mom	Mamma	Sun	Sole
Dad	Babbo	Better	Migliore
Brother	Fratello	Worse	Peggiore
Sister	Sorella	Beautiful	Bello
Cousin	Cugino	Real	Reale
Grandfather	Nonno	Easy	Facile
Grandmother	Nonna	Hard	Duro
Please	Per favore	Next	Prossimo
Thank you	Ringraziarla	One	Un
Sorry	Dispiace, Spiacente	Two	Due
New	Nuovo	Three	Tre
Inside	L'interno	Four	Quattro
Outside	L'esterno	Five	Cinque
Different	Diverso	Six	Sei
First	Primo	Seven	Sette
Last	L'ultimo	Eight	Otto
Child	Il bambino	Nine	Nove
Man	L'uomo	Ten	Dieci
Women	Le donne	Number	Numero
Week	La settimana	Month	Mese

To Talk	Parlare	**To Drive**	Guidare
To Walk	Camminare	**To Pay**	Pagare
To Run	Correre	**To Buy**	Comprare
To Sleep	Dormire	**To Practice**	Praticare
To Begin	Iniziare	**To Prepare**	Preparare
To Finish	Finire	**To Meet**	Incontrare
To Drink	Bere	**To Fly**	Volare
To Smoke	Fumare	**To Visit**	Visitare
To Prefer	Preferire	**To Swim**	Nuotare
To Loose	Allentare	**To Show**	Mostrare
To Forget	Dimenticare	**To Know**	Sapere
To Hold	Tenere	**To Think**	Pensare
To Follow	Seguire	**To Believe**	Credere
To Continue	Continuare	**To Love**	Amare
To Want	Volere	**To Like**	Amare
To Stay	Stare	**To Use**	Usare
To Keep	Tenere	**To Try**	Tentare
To Play	Giocare	**To Understand**	Capire
To Get	Prendere	**To Have**	Avere
To Help	Aiutare	**To Happen**	Succedere
To Go	Andare	**To Recognize**	Riconoscere
To Give	Dare	**To Hear**	Sentire
To Receive	Ricevere	**To Listen**	Ascoltare
To Bring	Portare	**To Press**	Premere
To Work	Lavorare	**To Promise**	Promettere
To Hope	Sperare	**To Choose**	Scegliere
To Live	Vivere.	**To Arrive**	Arrivare
To Find	Trovare	**To Leave**	Partire
To Look	Guardare	**To Leave {Something}**	Lasciare
To Search	Ricercare	**To Do**	Fare
To See	Vedere	**To Order**	Ordinare
To Read	Leggere	**To Pretend**	Fingere
To Write	Scrivere	**To Change**	Cambiare
To Learn	Imparare	**I Can**	Posso
To Teach	Insegnare	**To Return**	Ritornare
To Take	Portare	**To Borrow**	Prendere
To Turn on	Accendere	**To Sit**	Sedere
To Turn off	Spegnere	**To Need**	Avere bisogno
To Close	Chiudere	**To Say**	Dire
To Put	Mettere	**To Remove**	Togliere
To Allow	Consentire	**To Travel**	Viaggiare
To Lift	Sollevare	**To Eat**	Mangiare
To Open	Aprire	**To Exchange**	Scambiare
To Wish	Desiderare	**To Mix**	Mescolare
To Enter	Entrare	**To Belong**	Appartenere
To Come	Venire	**To Feel**	Sentire
To Move	Muovere	**To Stop**	Fermare
To Rent	Affittare	**To Ask**	Chiedere
To Remember	Ricordare	**To Answer**	Rispondere
To Check	Controllare	**To Decide**	Decidere
To Call	Chiamare	**To Sell**	Vendere
To Resemble	Assomigliare	**To Wait**	L'attesa

Building Bridges

I Can	Posso
I Do	Faccio
I Go	Vado
I Need	Ho bisogno
I Want	Voglio
I See	Vedo
I Like	Amo
I Say	Dico
I Talk	Parlo

Phrases

I live in Miami
Io vivo a Miami
Io {I} vivo {live} a {in} Miami

Can you speak faster
Può parlare più veloce
Può {Can you} parlare {speak} più {more} veloce {faster}

I'm sorry, I don't speak English very well
Mi dispiace, ma non parlo bene inglesi
Mi {I am} dispiace {Sorry}, ma {I} non {no} parlo {speak} bene {good} inglesi {English}

Italian Pronuncaiton

C – ch
Ch – k
G – j
Gh – g
Gl – ly
Gn – ny
H – (silent)
Sc – sh
Z, zz – ts, dz
U – oo

For the Italian language; grammar, pronunciation, accent, conjugation, reading, and sentence structure are recommended but not required for non-Shakespearean speakers.

Brazilian Portuguese

Portuguese has over 200 million native speakers, as it is the sixth most common language in the world. The language originated from Latin roots, and became popular after a Roman invasion, which spread the language to other parts of the area. The incoming Romans blended their language with that of the natives, so Portuguese began to modify. Traders of the time began to use the language, so it spread rapidly, making its way into Africa and Asia. In fact, before the language was officially modernized, it was more unique. Today, there are more traces of Greek and Latin and fewer words from the actual Portuguese language. Although the dialect in this book more closely resembles the dialect of Portugal than the Brazilian dialect, nonetheless the dialects from both countries are almost 100% similar.

Spoken in: Portugal, Brazil, Angola, Mozambique, and several other CPLP countries

I	Eu
Me	Eu
My	Meu
Mine	Mina
His	Dele
Him	Ele
Her	Ela
Hers	Dela
He	Ele
She	Ela
Us	Nós
Our	Nosso
With you	Com você
With You {Plural}	Com Vocês
With her	Com ela
With him	Com ele
With Them	Com eles
Without me	Sem mim
Without	Sem
Without you	Sem você
Without you {Plural}	Sem vocês
Them, They	Eles
Their	Seu
You	Você
You {Plural}	Vocês
I am	Eu sou
I was	Eu era
I will	Vou ir
Are you	É você
We	Nós
Without her	Sem ela
Without Them	Sem eles
Without Him	Sem ele
With me	Com mim
For you	Para você
To be	A ser
Yours	Seu
We are	Somos
With us	Conosco
Without us	Sem nós
Who	Quem

What	Que	Something	Algo
If	Se	Sometimes	Às vezes
Similar	Similar	Somewhere	Em algum lugar
Where	Onde	Yes	Sim
Were	Eram	No	Não
When	Quando	Less	Menos
Only	Somente	Instead	Preferivelmente
Was	Era	Including	Incluir
Other	Outro	While	Quando
Since	Desde	Someone	Alguém
Same	Mesmos que	Again	Outra vez
With	Com	Away	Afastado
Already	Já	But	Mas
Together	Junto	Don't	Não
Then	Então	Both	Ambos
Than	Do que	Because	Porque
More	Mais	Still, Yet	Ainda
Very	Muito	Time	Tempos
Much, a lot	Muito	Time	Tempo
From	De	Time	Hora
And	E	Also, Too	Também
Before	Antes	Around	Ao redor
After	Após	Never	Nunca
Afterwards	De mais tarde	Of course	Claro
To	A	Here	Aqui
The	La	This	Isto
That	Isso	OK	Okay
That	Que	Just	Apenas
Is	É	Although	Embora
Which	Que	Through	Através
For	Para	It is	É
Of	De	Everywhere	Em toda parte
Against	Contra	Ready	Não apronta
Always	Sempre	Soon	Logo
Until	Até	Except	Exceto
Everything	Tudo	Between	No meio
Every	Cada	Now	Agora
Even If	Nivele Se	Later	Mais tarde
Things	Coisas	Toward	Para
There	Lá	How Much & How Many	Quanto
Into	Em	Neither	Nenhuns
Or	Ou	None	Nenhum
On	Em	Nobody	Ninguém
About	Sobre	Maybe	Talvez
How	Como	Way	Maneira
In	Dentro	Why	Porque
Nothing	O nada	Side	O lado
At	Em	Everybody	Todo o mundo
Almost	Quase	A Few	Alguns

Small	Pequeno	Name	Nome
Big	Grande	Last name	Sobre Nome
Hot	Quente	What is you name	Qual seu nome
Cold	Frio	How old are you	Cuan o anos você tem
Up	Acima	Welcome	Boa vinda
Down	Baixo	Years	Anos
Person	Pessoa	Sky	Céu
People	Pessoas	Night	Noite
Fast	Rápido	Light	Luz
Slow	Lento	Darkness	Escuridão
Day	Dia	Morning	Manhã
Tomorrow	Amanhã	House	Casa
Today	Hoje	Car	Carro
Yesterday	Ontem	Left	Esquerdo
Good	Bom	Right	Direita
Bad	Mal	Place	Lugar
Hello	Oi	Straight	Reto
Goodbye	Adeus	Parents	Pais
How are you	Como você estar	Book	Livro
Nice to meet you	Prazer conocer	Problem	Problema
Good Night	Boa Noite	Behind	Atrás
Good evening	Boa tarde	In-Front	Em-Dianteiro
Good Morning	Bom Dia	Close	Cercar
Friend	Amigo	Far	Distante
Mom	Mae	Sun	Sol
Dad	Pai	Better	Melhor
Brother	Irmão	Worse	Mais mau
Sister	Irmã	Beautiful	Bonito
Cousin	Primo	Real	Real
Grandfather	Avô	Easy	Fácil
Grandmother	Avó	Hard	Duramente
Please	Por favor	Next	Próximo
Thank you	Obrigado	One	Um
Sorry	Pesaroso	Two	Dois
New	Novo	Three	Três
Inside	Interior	Four	Quatro
Outside	Exterior	Five	Cinco
Different	Diferente	Six	Seis
First	Primeiramente	Seven	Sete
Last	Último	Eight	Oito
Child	Criança	Nine	Nove
Man	Homem	Ten	Dez
Women	Mulheres	Number	Numere
Month	Mês	Week	Semana

To Talk	Falar	To Drive	Conducir
To Walk	Andar	To Pay	Pagar
To Run	Correr	To Buy	Comprar
To Sleep	Dormir	To Practice	Praticar
To Begin	Começar	To Prepare	Preparar
To Finish	Terminar	To Meet	Encontrar
To Drink	Beber	To Fly	Voar
To Smoke	Fumar	To Visit	Visitar
To Prefer	Preferir	To Swim	Nadar
To Loose	Afrouxar	To Show	Mostrar
To Forget	Esquecer	To Know	Saber
To Hold	Prender	To Think	Pensar
To Follow	Seguir	To Believe	Acreditar
To Continue	Continuar	To Love	Amar
To Want	Querer	To Like	Gostar
To Stay	Permanecer	To Use	Usar
To Keep	Manter	To Try	Tentar
To Play	Jogar	To Understand	Entender
To Get	Começar	To Have	Ter
To Help	Ajudar	To Happen	Acontecer
To Go	Ir	To Recognize	Reconhecer
To Give	Dar	To Hear	Ouvir
To Receive	Receber	To Listen	Escutar
To Bring	Trazer	To Press	Pressionar
To Work	Trabalhar	To Promise	Prometer
To Hope	Esperar	To Choose	Escolher
To Live	Viver	To Arrive	Chegar
To Find	Encontrar	To Leave	Partir
To Look	Olhar	To Leave {Something}	Deixar
To Search	Procurarar	To Do	Fazer
To See	Ver	To Order	Mandar
To Read	Ler	To Pretend	Fingir
To Write	Escrever	To Change	Mudar
To Learn	Aprender	I Can	Posso
To Teach	Ensinar	To Return	Retornar
To Take	Colher	To Borrow	Emprestar
To Turn on	Virar em	To Sit	Sentar
To Turn off	Desligar	To Need	Necessitar
To Close	Fechar	To Say	Dizer
To Put	Pôr	To Remove	Retirar
To Allow	Reservar	To Travel	Viajar
To Lift	Levantar	To Eat	Comer
To Enter	Entrar	To Exchange	Trocar
To Wish	Desejar	To Mix	Misturar
To Enter	Entrar	To Belong	Pertencer
To Come	Vir	To Feel	Sentir-se
To Move	Mover	To Stop	Parar
To Rent	Alugar	To Ask	Pedir
To Remember	Lembrar	To Answer	Responder
To Check	Verificar	To Decide	Decidir
To Call	Chamar	To Sell	Vender
To Resemble	Azemblar	To Wait	Esperar

Building Bridges

I Can	Posso
I Do	Faço
I Go	Vou
I Need	Necessito
I Want	Quero
I See	Vejo
I Like	Gosto
I Say	Digo
I Talk	Falo

Pode {please} **falar** {speak} **mais** {more} **Rápido** {faster}?
Please speak faster.

Onde **{where}** gostarian **{will they like}** de **{for}** ir **{to go}**?
Where will they like to go?

Reading {same as in Spanish}:
"Ñ" is pronounced as {ny}, for example Mañana {morning}, it sounds like {ma-ny-ana}
"LL" is pronounced as {je} for example llegar {to arrive}, it sounds like {je-gar}
"Y" is pronounced as {ie} for example y {and}, it sounds like {ie}
"J" is pronounced as {h - and depending on the word that comes after then it will be "he" "hu" "ha"} for example mujer {woman}, it sounds like {mu-he-r}
"Ã " is pronounced as {aa} for example Não {no}, it sounds like {n-aa-o}
"Ç" is pronounced as "Se"

For the Portuguese language; grammar, pronunciation, accent, conjugation, reading, and sentence structure are recommended but not required for non-Shakespearean speakers. Portuguese and Spanish are extremely similar therefore Spanish speakers can pick up on the language faster than others, and vice versa.

Portuguese Pronunciation

Ã – is nasalized (aa)

É – like "get"

Ê – like "they"

Ó – (o like in shop)

Ô - (o like in pole)

Ú – (silent)

GÜ, Ü– (gÜe gÜi like g in English "got")

Ãe – y

Ão – ow

OÊ– oi (coin)

Ç – s (sit)

Ch - sh

H – (silent)

J – s

Nh – ni

Ao - ow

Eu – (both vowels pronounced separately)

Spanish

Though the term "Spanish" is deemed the languages' more modern form, many countries in South America, including Paraguay, Bolivia, Uruguay, Ecuador, Argentina, Peru and Chile refer to it is "Castellano." Spanish originated in Spain, and it closely resembled Portuguese and Latin. Most of the speakers of these three languages find it simple to translate each other's languages, since they all stem from the same source. The Spanish language was spread during the 1500's by Spanish colonists, coming from Spain to South America. Since then, the language has grown to now be one of the official languages of the United Nations and the fourth most spoken language in the world. Spanish is still rising in popularity, as it has 98 million non-native speakers and 402 million native speakers.

Spoken in: Argentina, Bolivia, Chile, Colombia, Costa Rica, Cuba, Dominican Republic, Ecuador, El Salvador, Equatorial Guinea, European Union, Guatemala, Honduras, Mexico, Nicaragua, N ew Mexico (USA), Panama, Paraguay, Peru, Puerto Rico, Spain, Uruguay, and Venezuela.

I	Yo
Me	Yo
My	Mí
Mine	Mio
His	De el - su
Him	El
Her	De ella – su
Hers	De ella
He	El
She	Ella
Us	Nosotros
Our	De Nosotros – nuestro
With you	Contigo
With You {Plural}	Con ustedes
With her	Con ella
With him	Con él
With Them	Con ellos
Without me	Sin mí
Without	Sin
Without you	Sin ti
Without you {Plural}	Sin ustedes
Them	Ellos
Their	De ellos – Sus
You	Tu, te, ti
You {Plural}	Ustedes
I am	Soy
I was	Estuve
I will	Sere
Are you	Eres
They	Ellos
Without her	Sin ella
Without Them	Sin ellos
Without Him	Sin el
With me	Conmigo
For you	Para ti
To be	Ser, estar
Yours	Sus
We are	Somos
With us	Con nosotros
Without us	Sin nosotros
Who	Quien

What	Qué	Something	Algo
If	Si	Sometimes	Algunas veces
Similar	Como	Somewhere	Alguna lugar
Where	Donde	Yes	Sí
Were	Fueron	No	No
When	Cuando	Less	Menos
Only	Sólamente	Instead	Enves
Was	Era	Including	Inclullendo
Other	Otro	While	Mientras
Since	Desde	Someone	Alguien
Same	Mismo	Again	Vuelve, Otra ves
With	Con	Away	Lejos
Already	Ya	But	Pero
Together	Juntos	Don't	No
Then	Entonces	Both	Ambos
Than	Que	Because	Porque
More	Más	Still, Yet	Todavía, aun
Very	Muy	Time	Veces
Much, a lot	Mucho	Time	Tiempo
From	Del	Time	Hora
And	Y	Also, Too	También
Before	Antes	Around	Alrededor
After	Después	Never	Nunca
Afterwards	Luego	Of course	Por supuesto
To	Al	Here	Aquí
The	El, la	This	Esto
That	Eso	OK	De acuerdo
That	Que	Just	Apenas
Is	Es	Although	Aunque
Which	Cual	Through	Atra ves
For	Para	It is	Hay
Of	De	Everywhere	Todas partes
Against	Contra	Ready	Listo
Always	Siempre	Soon	Pronto
Until	Hasta	Except	Excepto
Everything	Todo	Between	Entre
Every	Todo	Now	Ya
Even If	Incluso	Later	En la Tarde
Things	Cosas	Toward	Hacia
There	Allí	How Much & How Many	Cuanto
Into	Adentro	Neither	Tampoco
Or	O	None	Ninguno
On	Sobre	Nobody	Nadie
About	Acerca	Maybe	Quizá, tal vez
How	Cómo	Way	Manera
In	En	Why	Por qué
Nothing	Nada	Side	Lado
At	En	Everybody	Todos
Almost	Casi	A Few	Pocos

Small	Pequeño	**Name**	Nombre
Big	Grande, gran	**Last name**	Apellido
Hot	Caliente	**What is your name**	Cual es tu nombre
Cold	Frío	**How old are you**	Cuántos años tiene
Up	Arriba	**Welcome**	Bienvenido
Down	Abajo	**Years**	Años
Person	Persona	**Sky**	Cielo
People	Gente	**Night**	Noche
Fast	Rápido	**Light**	Luz
Slow	Despacio, lento	**Darkness**	Obscuridad
Day	Día	**Morning**	Mañana
Tomorrow	Mañana	**House**	Casa
Today	Ahoy	**Car**	Carro
Yesterday	Ayer	**Left**	Izquierda
Good	Bueno	**Right**	Derecha
Bad	Malo	**Place**	Lugar
Hello	Hola	**Straight**	Derecho
Goodbye	Chao	**Parents**	Padres
How are you	Como estas	**Book**	Libro
Nice to meet you	Mucho gusto	**Problem**	Problema
Good Night	Buenas noche	**Behind**	Atrás
Good Afternoon	Buenas tardes	**In-Front**	Enfrente
Good Morning	Buenas dia	**Close**	Cercar
Friend	Amigo {ga)	**Far**	Lejos
Mom	Mamá	**Sun**	Sol
Dad	Papá	**Better**	Mejor
Brother	Hermano	**Worse**	Peor
Sister	Hermana	**Beautiful**	Lindo
Cousin	Primo	**Real**	Real
Grandfather	Abuelo	**Easy**	Fácil
Grandmother	Abuela	**Hard**	Dificil
Please	Por favor	**Next**	Próximo
Thank you	Gracias	**One**	Uno
Sorry	Lo siento	**Two**	Dos
New	Nuevo	**Three**	Tres
Inside	Adentro	**Four**	Quatro
Outside	Afuera	**Five**	Cinco
Different	Diferente	**Six**	Sies
First	Primer	**Seven**	Siete
Last	Ultimo	**Eight**	Ocho
Child	Hijo	**Nine**	Nueve
Man	Hombre	**Ten**	Dies
Women	Mujer	**Number**	Número
Week	Semana	**Month**	Mes

To Talk	Hablar	**To Drive**	Manejar
To Walk	Caminar	**To Pay**	Pagar
To Run	Correr	**To Buy**	Comprar
To Sleep	Dormir	**To Practice**	Practicar
To Begin	Comenzar	**To Prepare**	Preparar
To Finish	Acabar	**To Meet**	Conocer
To Drink	Beber	**To Fly**	Volar
To Smoke	Fumar	**To Visit**	Visitar
To Prefer	Preferir	**To Swim**	Nadar
To Loose	Perder	**To Show**	Mostrar
To Forget	Olvidar	**To Know**	Saber
To Hold	Sostener	**To Think**	Penzar
To Follow	Seguir	**To Believe**	Creer
To Continue	Continuar	**To Love**	Amar
To Want	Querer	**To Like**	Gustar
To Stay	Quedar	**To Use**	Usar
To Keep	Guardar	**To Try**	Tratar
To Play	Jugar	**To Win**	Ganar
To Get	Consigar	**To Have**	Tener
To Help	Ayudar	**To Happen**	Occurir
To Go	Ir	**To Recognize**	Reconocer
To Give	Dar	**To Hear**	Oir
To Receive	Recibir	**To Listen**	Escuchar
To Bring	Traer	**To Press**	Oprimir
To Work	Trabajar	**To Promise**	Prometer
To Hope	Esperar	**To Choose**	Escoger
To Live	Vivir	**To Arrive**	Llegar
To Find	Encontrar	**To Leave**	Salir
To Look	Mirar	**To Leave {Something}**	Dejar
To Search	Buscar	**To Do**	Hacer
To See	Ver	**To Order**	Ordenar
To Read	Leer	**To Pretend**	Pretender
To Write	Escribir	**To Change**	Cambiar
To Learn	Aprender	**I Can**	Yo Puedo
To Teach	Enseñar	**To Return**	Regrezar
To Take	Recoger	**To Borrow**	Pedir prestado
To Turn on	Encender	**To Sit**	Sentar
To Turn off	Apagar	**To Need**	Necesitar
To Close	Cerrar	**To Say**	Decir
To Put	Poner	**To Remove**	Sacar
To Allow	Permitir	**To Travel**	Viajar
To Lift	Levantar	**To Eat**	Comer
To Open	Abrir	**To Exchange**	Intercambiar
To Wish	Desear	**To Mix**	Mesclar
To Enter	Entrar	**To Belong**	Pertenecer
To Come	Venir	**To Feel**	Sentir
To Move	Mover	**To Stop**	Detener, parar
To Rent	Alquilar	**To Ask**	Pedir
To Remember	Recordar	**To Answer**	Contestar
To Check	Revizar	**To Decide**	Decidir
To Call	Llamar	**To Sell**	Vender
To Resemble	Parecer	**To Wait**	Esperar

Building Bridges

I Can	Puedo
I Do	Hago
I Go	Voy
I Need	Necesito
I Want	Quiero
I See	Veo
I Like	Gusto
I Say	Digo
I Talk	Hablo

Phrases:

I need to talk to you

Necesito Hablar contigo

Necesito {I need} Hablar {to talk} contigo {with you}

I want to go home

Yo quiero ir a casa

Yo {I} quiero {[I] want} ir {to go} a {to} casa {house}

Can you please check what I did

Por favor, tu puedes revizar que hice

Por favor {please}, tu {you} puedes {[you] can} revisar
{to check} que {what} hice {I did}

Reading and Pronunciation in Spanish

C is pronounced "th"

G followed by "e,i" is pronounced as kh, like the British Loch

H is silent

J is pronounced as kh, like the British Loch

Ñ is pronounced as {ny}, for example Mañana {morning}, it sounds like {ma-ny-ana}

LL is pronounced as {je} for example llegar {to arrive}, it sounds like {je-gar}

Y is pronounced as {ie} for example y {and}, it sounds like {ie}

V is pronounced as "b"

Z is pronounced as "th"

For the Spanish language; grammar, pronunciation, accent, conjugation, reading, and sentence structure are recommended but not required for non-Shakespearean speakers. Spanish and Portuguese are extremely similar therefore Portuguese speakers can pick up on the language faster than others, and vice versa.

European Languages

Section II: Germanic Languages

- Dutch
- German
- Norwegian

Dutch

Spoken by approximately 22 million people worldwide, Dutch is the official language of Belgium, the Netherlands and Suriname. The language originated from Old Dutch, which was spoken by the Franks hundreds of years ago. The German language is similar to Dutch as well. The actual term "Dutch" is actually derived from a German word, which was later translated to the Latin work "theodisk," which means, "of the people." Dutch is also a part of the Western Germanic language branch. Because of their similarity, some people can effortlessly speak both languages, as well as read in corresponding texts.

Spoken in: Netherlands, Belgium, Suriname, Aruba, Netherlands Antilles, South Africa.

I	Ik
Me	Mij
My	Mijn
Mine	Mijn
His	Van Hem
Him	Hem
Her	Haar
Hers	Van haar
He	Hij
She	Zij
Us	Wy
Our	Ons
With you	Met u
With You {Plural}	Met de jullie
With her	Met haar
With him	Met hem
With Them	Met hun
Without	Zonder
Without me	Zonder mij
Without you	Zonder u
Without you {Plural}	Zonder jou
Them, They	Hun
Their	Hun
You	U
You {Plural}	Jullie
I am	Ik ben
I was	Ik Ben geweest
I will	Ik wil
Are you	Bent u
We	Wij
Without her	Zonder haar
Without Them	Zonder hun
Without Him	Zonder hem
With me	Met my
For You	Voor u
To be	Ie zyn
Yours	Voorjou
We are	Wij zijn
With us	Met ons
Without us	Zonder ons
Who	Wie

What	Wat	**Something**	Iets
If	Als	**Sometimes**	Soms
Similar	Gelijkaardig	**Somewhere**	Ergens
Where	Waar	**Yes**	Ja
Were	Waren	**No**	Nee
When	Toen	**Less**	Minder
Only	Allen maar	**Instead**	In plaats daarvan
Was	Was	**Including**	Het omvatten
Other	Andere	**While**	Terwijl
Since	Sinds	**Someone**	Iemand
Same	Zelfde zoals	**Again**	Opnieuw
With	Met	**Away**	Weg
Already	Al	**But**	Maar
Together	Samen	**Don't**	Niet
Then	Toen	**Both**	Allebei
Than	Dan	**Because**	Omdat
More	Meer	**Still, Yet**	Nog
Very	Zeer	**Time**	Keer
Much, a lot	Veel	**Time**	Tijd
From	Van	**Time**	Uur
And	En	**Also, Too**	Ook
Before	Vóór	**Around**	Rond
After	Na	**Never**	Nooit
Afterwards	Daarna	**Of course**	Natuurlyk
To	Aan	**Here**	Hier
The		**This**	Dit
That	Dat	**OK**	O.K.
That	Dat	**Just**	Enkel
Is	Is	**Although**	Hoewel
Which	Welke	**Through**	Door
For	Voor	**It is**	Is
Of	Van	**Everywhere**	Overal
Against	Tegen	**Ready**	Klaar
Always	Altijd	**Soon**	Spoedig
Until	Tot dat	**Except**	Accepteer
Everything	Alles	**Between**	Tussen
Every	Elke	**Now**	Nu
Even If	Ook als	**Later**	Later
Things	Dingen	**Toward**	Naar
There	Daar	**How Much**	Hoeveel
Into	In	**Neither**	Geen van beiden
Or	Of	**None**	Niets
On	Op	**Nobody**	Niemand
About	Ongeveer	**Maybe**	Misschien
How	Hoe	**Way**	Manier
In	Binnen	**Why**	Waarom
Nothing	Niets	**Side**	Kant
At	Bij	**Everybody**	Iedereen
Almost	Bijna	**A Few**	Een paar

Small	Klein	**Name**	Naam
Big	Groot	**Last name**	Laatste naam
Hot	Heet	**What is you name**	Wat is ie naam
Cold	Koud	**How old are you**	Hoe oud ben je
Up	Op	**Welcome**	Welkom
Down	Onder	**Years**	Jaaren
Person	Persoon	**Sky**	De hemel
People	Mensen	**Night**	Nacht
Fast	Snel	**Light**	Licht
Slow	Langzaam	**Darkness**	Juiste Duisternis
Day	Dag	**Morning**	Morgen
Tomorrow	Morgen	**House**	Huis
Today	Vandaag	**Car**	Auto
Yesterday	Gisteren	**Left**	Links
Good	Goed	**Right**	Recht
Bad	Slecht	**Place**	Plaats
Hello	Hello	**Straight**	Rechtstreeks
Goodbye	Vaarwel	**Parents**	Ouders
How are you	Hoe gaat	**Book**	Het
Nice to meet you	Leuk je te ontmoeten	**Problem**	Leuk jete ontmoeten
Good Night	Goede Nacht	**Behind**	Achter
Good Afternoon	Goede Middag	**Front**	Voorzijde
Good Morning	Goede Morgen	**Near**	Nabij
Friend	Vriend	**Far**	Ver
Mom	Mam	**Sun**	Zon
Dad	Papa	**Better**	Beter
Brother	Broer	**Worse**	Slechter
Sister	Zuster	**Beautiful**	Mooi
Cousin	Neef, nicht	**Real**	Echt
Grandfather	Grootvader	**Easy**	Gemakkelijk
Grandmother	Grootmoeder	**Hard**	Hard
Please	Aistublieft	**Next**	Daarna
Thank you	Dank u	**One**	Één
Sorry	Sorry	**Two**	Twee
New	Nieuw	**Three**	Drie
Inside	Binnenkant	**Four**	Vier
Outside	Buiten	**Five**	Vijf
Different	Verschillende	**Six**	Zes
First	Eerst	**Seven**	Zeven
Last	Duur	**Eight**	Acht
Child	Kind	**Nine**	Negen
Man	Man	**Ten**	Tien
Women	Vrouwen	**Number**	Nummer
Week	Week	**Month**	Mand

To Talk	Praten	**To Drive**	Ryden
To Walk	Te lopen	**To Pay**	Om te betalen
To Run	Te lopen	**To Buy**	Kopen
To Sleep	Slapen	**To Practice**	Praktijk
To Begin	Beginnen	**To Prepare**	Voorbereidingen
To Finish	Eindigen	**To Meet**	Animoeten
To Drink	Drinken	**To Fly**	Vliegen
To Smoke	Te roken	**To Visit**	Te bezoeken
To Prefer	Verkiezen	**To Swim**	Zwemmen
To Loose	Maken	**To Show**	Te laten zien
To Forget	Vergeten	**To Know**	Te laten weten
To Hold	Houden	**To Think**	Om te denken
To Follow	Volgen	**To Believe**	Geloven
To Continue	Verder te gaan	**To Love**	Om te houden
To Want	om te willen	**To Like**	Houden van
To Stay	Om te blijven	**To Use**	Om te gebruiken
To Keep	Houden	**To Try**	Om te proberen
To Play	Te spelen	**To Understand**	Begrijpen
To Get	Krijgen	**To Have**	Hebben
To Help	Om te helpen	**To Happen**	Om te gebeuren
To Go	Te gaan	**To Recognize**	Se herken
To Give	Geven	**To Hear**	Te horen
To Receive	te ontvangen	**To Listen**	Te luisteren
To Bring	Brengen	**To Press**	Om te drukken
To Work	Om te werken	**To Promise**	Om te beloven
To Hope	Hopen	**To Choose**	Om te kiezen
To Live	Te leven	**To Arrive**	Aan te komen
To Find	Te vinden	**To Leave**	Weg te gaan
To Look	Te kijken	**To Leave**	Letfn
To Search	Zoeken	**To Do**	Doen
To See	Om te zien	**To Order**	Te orderen
To Read	Te lezen	**To Pretend**	Beweren
To Write	Om te schrijven	**To Change**	Veranderen
To Learn	Leren	**I Can**	Ik kan
To Teach	Om te onderwijzen	**To Return**	Terug te keren
To Take	Nemen	**To Borrow**	Lenen
To Turn on	Om aan te zetten	**To Sit**	Zitten
To Turn off	Om uit te zetten	**To Need**	Gebruiken
To Close	Te pichtby	**To Say**	Zeggen
To Put	Om te zetten	**To Remove**	Verwijderen
To allow	Toestaan	**To Travel**	Op Reis
To Lift	Om op te heffen	**To Eat**	Eten
To Open	Openen	**To Exchange**	Ruilen
To Wish	Dit te wensen	**To Mix**	Mengen
To Enter	Binnengaan	**To Belong**	Behoren
To Come	Om te komen	**To Feel**	Voelen
To Move	Te bewegen	**To Stop**	Stoppen
To Rent	Te Huren	**To Ask**	Vragen
To Remember	Zich te herinneren	**To Answer**	Antwoorden
To Check	Om te controleren	**To Decide**	Beslisen
To Call	Te bellen	**To Sell**	Vervreemden
To Resemble	Te lijken	**To Wait**	Wachten

Building Bridges

I Can	Ik Kan
I Do	Ik Doe
I Go	Ik Ga
I Need	Ik Gebruik
I Want	Ik Wil
I See	Ik Zie
I Like	Ik Hou van
I Say	Ik Zeg
I Talk	Ik Prat

Wat {what} zei {say} u {you}? What did you say?

Dat {that} is {is} beter {better}. That's better.

Ik {I} begrijp {understand} u {you} als {if} u {you} langzaam {slowly} praat {speak}. I understand you if you speak slowly.

Begrijpt {understand} u {you}? Do you understand?

Prat {speak} u {you} Engels {English}? Do you prat English?

Prat {speak} er Iedereen {everyone} Engels {English} hier {here}? Does everyone here speak English?

For the Dutch language; grammar, pronunciation, accent, conjugation, reading, and sentence structure are recommended but not required for non-Shakespearean speakers.

German

The German language was first used during the Habsburg Empire, located in Eastern Europe. Spoken by the common people of the time, the language was used more for economic trading and business. Though the Empire fell well over 100 years ago, German remains one of ten most common languages, as it is spoken by over 120 million people. It is the official language of Germany, as well as one of twenty of the European Union. However, it is also spoken in various other countries, like Poland, Italy, Denmark and Belgium, Switzerland and Austria. The language is spoken more frequently by European natives than French is, as 13.3% of Europe's population uses the language daily.

Spoken in: Germany, Austria, Switzerland, Liechtenstein, Belgium, Luxembourg, Netherlands

I	Ich
Me	Mir, mich
My	Mein
Mine	mein
His	Seine
Him	Ihm
Her	Ihre
Hers	Ihrs
He	Er
She	Sie
Us	Uns
Our	Unser
With you	Mit dir
With You {Plural}	Mit Ihnen
With her	Mit ihr
With him	Mit ihm
With Them	Mit ihnen
Without me	Ohne mich
Without	Ohne
Without you	Ohne Sie
Without you {Plural}	Ohne dich
Them, They	Sie
Their	Ihr
You	Du
You {Plural}	Sie
I am	Ich bin
I was	Ich war
I will	Ich Wille
Are you	Bist du
We	
Without her	Ohne sie
Without Them	Ohne sie
Without Him	Ohne ihn
With me	Mit mir
For you	Für Sie
To be	Zu sein
Yours	Ihres
We are	Wir sind
With us	Mit uns
Without us	Ohne uns
Who	Wer

What	Was	**Something**	Etwas
If	Wenn	**Sometimes**	Manchmal
Similar	Ähnlich	**Somewhere**	Irgendwo
Where	Wo	**Yes**	Ja
Were	Waren	**No**	Nein
When	Wenn	**Less**	Weniger
Only	Nur	**Instead**	Anstatt
Was	War	**Including**	Einschließend
Other	Anderes	**While**	Während
Since	Seit dem	**Someone**	Jemand
Same	Selbe	**Again**	Wieder
With	Mit	**Away**	Weg
Already	Bereits	**But**	Aber
Together	Zusammen	**Don't**	Tue nicht
Then	Dann	**Both**	Beide
Than	Als	**Because**	Weil
More	Mehr	**Still, Yet**	Noch
Very	Sehr	**Time**	Mal
Much, a lot	Viel	**Time**	Zeit
From	Von	**Time**	Stunde
And	Und	**Also, Too**	Auch
Before	Vorher	**Around**	Um
After	Nachher	**Never**	Nie
Afterwards	Danach	**Of course**	Selbstverständlich
To	Zu	**Here**	Hier
The	Der {M}, die {F}	**This**	Dieses
That	Der	**OK**	OKAY
That	Daß	**Just**	Gerade
Is	Ist	**Although**	Obwohl
Which	Welches	**Through**	Durch
For	Für	**It is**	Er ist
Of	Von	**Everywhere**	Überall
Against	Gegen	**Ready**	Fertig
Always	Immer	**Soon**	Bald
Until	Bis	**Except**	Außer
Everything	Alles	**Between**	Zwischen
Every	Jedes	**Now**	Jetzt
Even If	Sogan wenn	**Later**	Später
Things	Sache	**Toward**	In Richtung zu
There	Dort	**How Much & How Many**	Wie viel
Into	In	**Neither**	Weder
Or	Oder	**None**	Kein
On	Auf	**Nobody**	Niemand
About	ungefähr	**Maybe**	Möglicherweise
How	Wie	**Way**	Weg
In	Innen	**Why**	Warum
Nothing	Nichts	**Side**	Seite
At	Bei	**Everybody**	Jeder
Almost	Fast	**A Few**	Einige

Small	Klein	**Name**	Name
Big	Groß	**Last name**	Familien name
Hot	Heiß	**What is you name**	Wie heißen Sie?
Cold	Kalt	**How old are you**	Wie alt sind Sie?
Up	Herauf	**Welcome**	Willkommen
Down	Herunter	**Year**	Jahr
Person	Person	**Sky**	Himmel
People	Leute	**Night**	Nacht
Fast	Schnell	**Light**	Licht
Slow	Langsam	**Darkness**	Dunkelheit
Day	Tag	**Morning**	Morgen
Tomorrow	Morgen	**House**	Haus
Today	Heute	**Car**	Auto
Yesterday	Gestern	**Left**	Links
Good	Gut	**Right**	Recht
Bad	Schlecht	**Place**	Platz
Hello	Hallo	**Straight**	Gerade
Goodbye	Auf Wiedersehen	**Parents**	Eltern
How are you	Wie geht's	**Book**	Buch
Nice to meet you	Nett sie kennen zu lernen	**Problem**	Problem
Good Night	Gute Nacht	**Behind**	Hinter
Good Afternoon	Guter Nachmittag	**Front**	Vorne
Good Morning	Guter Morgen	**Near**	Nahe
Friend	Freund	**Far**	Weit
Mom	Mutter	**Sun**	Sonne
Dad	Vater	**Better**	Besser
Brother	Bruder	**Worst**	Am schlechtesten
Sister	Schwester	**Beautiful**	Schön
Cousin	Vetter	**Real**	Wirklich
Grandfather	Großvater	**Easy**	Leicht
Grandmother	Großmutter	**Hard**	Hart
Please	Bitte	**Next**	Nächste
Thank you	Danke	**One**	Ein
Sorry	Traurig	**Two**	Zwei
New	Neu	**Three**	Drei
Inside	Drinnen	**Four**	Vier
Outside	Draußen	**Five**	Fünf
Different	Verschieden	**Six**	Sechs
First	Zuerst	**Seven**	Sieben
Last	Zuletzt	**Eight**	Acht
Child	Kind	**Nine**	Neun
Man	Mann	**Ten**	Zehn
Women	Frau	**Number**	Zahl
Week	Woche	**Month**	Monat

To Talk	Sprechen	**To Drive**	Fahren
To Walk	Gehen	**To Pay**	Zahlen
To Run	Rennen	**To Buy**	Kaufen
To Sleep	Schlafen	**To Practice**	Zu üben
To Begin	Beginnen	**To Prepare**	Sich Vorbereiten
To Finish	Beenden	**To Meet**	Treffen
To Drink	Trinken	**To Fly**	Fliegen
To Smoke	Rauchen	**To Visit**	Besuchen
To Prefer	Bevorzugen	**To Swim**	Schwimmen
To Loose	Verlieren	**To Show**	Zeigen
To Forget	Vergessen	**To Know**	Wissen
To Hold	Halten	**To Think**	Denken
To Follow	Folgen	**To Believe**	Glauben
To Continue	Fortfahren	**To Love**	Lieben
To Want	Wünschen	**To Like**	Mag gerne
To Stay	Bleiben	**To Use**	Gebrauchen
To Keep	Halten	**To Try**	Versuchen
To Play	Spielen	**To Watch**	Aufpassen
To Get	Bekommen	**To Have**	Zu haben
To Help	Helfen	**To Happen**	Geschehen
To Go	Gehen	**To Recognize**	Erkennen
To Give	Geben	**To Hear**	Hören
To Receive	Empfangen	**To Listen**	Zuhören
To Bring	Bringen	**To Press**	Pressen
To Work	Arbeiten	**To Promise**	Versprechen
To Hope	Hoffen	**To Choose**	Wählen
To Live	Leben	**To Arrive**	Ankommen
To Find	Finden	**To Leave**	Verlassen
To Look	Schauen	**To Leave {Something}**	Liegen Lassen
To Search	Suchen	**To Do**	Tuen
To See	Sehen	**To Order**	Bestellen
To Read	Lesen	**To Pretend**	Vorzutäuschen
To Write	Schreiben	**To Change**	Ändern
To Learn	Erlernen	**I Can**	Können
To Teach	Unterrichten	**To Return**	Zurückgehen
To Take	Nehmen	**To Borrow**	Borgen
To Turn on	Anspornen	**To Sit**	Sitzen
To Turn off	Auslöschen	**To Need**	Brauchen
To Close	Schließen	**To Say**	Sagen
To Put	Hinstellen	**To Remove**	Entfernen
To Allow	Erlauben	**To Travel**	Reisen
To Lift	Heben	**To Eat**	Essen
To Open	Öffnen	**To Exchange**	Tauschen
To Wish	Wünschen	**To Mix**	Mischen
To Enter	Eintreten	**To Belong**	Zugehören
To Come	Kommen	**To Feel**	Fühlen
To Move	Bewegen	**To Stop**	Stoppen
To Rent	Mieten	**To Ask**	Fragen
To Remember	Erinnern	**To Answer**	Antworten
To Check	Überprüfen	**To Decide**	Entscheiden
To Call	Rufen, nennen	**To Sell**	Verkaufen
To Resemble	Ähneln	**To Wait**	Arten

Rules:
1- Adjectives come before the noun. All nouns begin with capital letters. The same word may be a verb or a noun, verb begins in small letter and noun in capital letter. Verbs are often divided into two parts and the last part is always at the end of a sentence, no matter how long.

There are 3 genders in German, Masculin, feminine and neuter. The adjective, which stands before the noun, must be in the same gender as the following noun. The articles before a noun are: der, die, das, dessen, dem, den. There is to be observed that also numbers ending go according to the following noun. Depending in which case the noun is used. There are four cases, Nominative, Genitive, Dative and Accusative.

Building Bridges

I Can	Ich Kann
I Do	Ich Mache
I Go	Ich Gehe
I Need	Ich Brauche
I Want	Ich möchte
I See	Ich Sehe
I Like	Ich Mag
I Say	Ich Sage
I Talk	Ich Rede

Reading
Au – ow
Ch – {refer back to introduction)
Sch – sh
Z - ts
Ää - ay
Öö - ooh
ß - ess {like double "S"}
Üü - uyuh

Sprichst {speak} **du** {you} **Deutsch** {German}
Do you speak German?

Können {can} **Sie** {you} **mir** {me} **helfen** {help}, **bitte** {please}
Can you help me, please

For the German language; grammar, pronunciation, accent, conjugation, reading, and sentence structure are recommended but not required for non-Shakespearean speakers. For the German language it's also recommended to learn how to pronounce the "ch" (refer back to introduction).

German Pronunciation

B – p
C – ts (before e,i,ä,ö,ts)
Ch – kh
Ch – k (before s)
D – t (end of word or between vowel and constant)
G – g
G – at end k (weg, vek)
J – y
W – v
S – z
ß – ss
Sch – sh
Tsch – ch
Tz – ts
V – f
Z – ts
Ö – vr
Y – ew
Ai, ay – ie
Au, - ow
äu, eu – oy

Norwegian

A part of the Scandinavian languages, Norwegian is the official language of Norway. It stemmed from the Old Norse language, which was actually at one point the most spoken language throughout Europe. However, Old Norse was spoken by Vikings, which settled in the Scandinavian Peninsula. As a result, the Old Norse language is evident in not only Norwegian, but Swedish and Danish as well. Since then, the language has evolved drastically. For example, Western and Eastern versions of Old Norse have emerged, as the Eastern version is found mostly in Denmark and the Western, in Norway, Greenland and Iceland. Over time, the two versions of Old Norse took separate paths, as the Western version evolved into Modern Norwegian.

Spoken in: Norway

I	Jeg
Me	Meg
My	Min
Mine	Mine
His	Hans
Him	Ham
Her	Henne
Hers	Hennes
He	Han
She	Hun
Us	Oss
Our	Vår
With you	Med deg
With You {Plural}	Med dere
With her	Med henne
With him	Med ham
With Them	Med Dem
Without me	Uten meg
Without	Uten
Without you	Uten Deg
Without you {Plural}	Uten dere
Them, They	Dem, de
Their	Deres
You	Du
You {Plural}	Dere
I am	Jeg er
I was	Jeg var
I will	Jeg vil
Are you	Er du {singular)
We	Vi
Without her	Uten henne
Without Them	Uten Dem
Without Him	Uten Ham
With me	Med meg
For you	For deg
To be	Være
Yours	Deres (sing: din)
We are	Vi er
With us	Med oss
Without us	Uten oss
Who	Hvem

What	Hva	**Something**	Noe
If	Om, hvis	**Sometimes**	Av og til
Similar	Liknende	**Somewhere**	Ett eller annet sted
Where	Hvor	**Yes**	Ja
Were	Var	**No**	Nei
When	Når	**Less**	Mindre
Only	Bare	**Instead**	Istedenfor
Was	Var	**Including**	Inkludert
Other	Andre *annen*	**While**	Mens
Since	Siden	**Someone**	Noen
Same as	Samme som	**Again**	Igjen
With	Med	**Away**	Borte
Already	Allerede	**But**	Men
Together	Sammen	**Don't**	Ikke
Then	Da	**Both**	Begge
Than	Enn	**Because**	Fordi
More	Mer	**Still, Yet**	Fortsatt
Very	Veldig	**Time**	Ganger
Much, a lot	Mye, masse	**Time**	Tiden
From	Fra	**Time**	Tid
And	Og	**Also, Too**	Også
Before	Før	**Around**	Rundt
After	Etter	**Never**	Aldri
Afterwards	Etterpå	**Of Course**	Selvfølgelig
To	Til	**Here**	Her
The	{no equivalent)	**This**	Dette
That	Det	**OK**	Greit
That	At	**Just**	Akkurat, bare
Is	Er	**Although**	Skjønt
Which	Som	**Through**	Gjennom
For	For	**It is**	Det er
Of	Av	**Everywhere**	Overalt
Against	Mot	**Ready**	Beredt, klar
Always	Alltid	**Soon**	Snart
Until	Til	**Except**	Unntatt
Everything	Alt	**Between**	Mellom
Every	Hver	**Now**	Nå
Even If	Selv om	**Later**	Senere
Things	Ting	**Toward**	Mot
There	Der	**How Much & How Many**	Hvor mye, & hvor mange
Into	Inn i	**Neither**	Verken
Or	Eller	**None**	Ingen
On	På	**Nobody**	Ingen
About	Omtrent, om	**Maybe**	Kanskje
How	Hvordan	**Way**	Måte
In	I	**Why**	Hvorfor
Nothing	Ingenting	**Side**	Side
At	På	**Everybody**	Alle
Almost	Nesten	**A Few**	Noen få

Small	Liten	Name	Navn
Big	Stor	Last name	Etternavn
Hot	Varm	What is your name	Hva heter du
Cold	Kald	How old are you	Hvor gammel er du
Up	Opp	Welcome	Velkommen
Down	Ned	Years	År
Person	Person	Sky	Himmel
People	Folk	Night	Natt
Fast	Fort	Light	Lys
Slow	Langsom	Darkness	Mørke
Day	Dag	Morning	Morgen
Tomorrow	I morgen	House	Hus
Today	I dag	Car	Bil
Yesterday	Igår	Left	Venstre
Good	God	Right	Høyre
Bad	Dårlig	Place	Sted
Hello	Hei	Straight	Rett
Goodbye	Ha det	Parents	Foreldre
How are you	Hvordan har du det	Book	Bok
Nice to meet you	Hyggelig å treffe deg	Problem	Problem
Good Night	God Natt	Behind	Bak
Good Afternoon	God ettermiddag	In-Front	Foran
Good Morning	God Morgen	Near	Nær
Friend	Venn	Far	Fjern
Mom	Mamma	Sun	Sol
Dad	Pappa	Better	Bedre
Brother	Bror	Worse	Verre
Sister	Søster	Beautiful	Vakker
Cousin	Søskenbarn	Real	Virkelig
Grandfather	Bestefar	Easy	Lett
Grandmother	Bestemor	Hard	Hard
Please	Vær så snill	Next	Neste
Thank you	Takk	One	En
Sorry	Unnskyld	Two	To
New	Ny	Three	Tre
Inside	Inne	Four	Fire
Outside	Ute	Five	Fem
Different	Forskjellig	Six	Seks
First	Først	Seven	Sju
Last	Sist	Eight	Åtte
Child	Barn	Nine	Ni
Man	Mann	Ten	Ti
Women	Kvinner	Number	Nummer
Week	Uke	Month	Måned

To Talk	Å Snakke	To Drive	Å Kjøre
To Walk	Å Gå	To Pay	Å Betale
To Run	Å Løpe	To Buy	Å Kjøpe
To Sleep	Å Sove	To Practice	Å Å øve
To Begin	Å Begynne	To Prepare	Å Forberede
To Finish	Å Avslutte	To Meet	Å Møtes
To Drink	Å Drikke	To Fly	Å fly
To Smoke	Å Røyke	To Visit	Å Besøke
To Prefer	Å Foretrekke	To Swim	Å Svømme
To Loose	Å Miste	To Show	Å Vise
To Forget	Å Glemme	To Know	Å Vite
To Hold	Å Holde	To Think	Å Tro, å anta
To Follow	Å Følge	To Believe	Å Tro
To Continue	Å Fortsette	To Love	Å Elske
To Want	Å Ville ha	To Like	Å like
To Stay	Å Bli	To Use	Å Bruke
To Keep	Å Beholde	To Try	Å Prøve
To Play	Å Leke	To Understand	Å Forstå
To Get	Å Få	To Have	Å Ha
To Help	Å Hjelpe	To Happen	Å hende
To Go	Å Dra	To Recognize	Å Anerkjenne
To Give	Å Gi	To Hear	Å Høre
To Receive	Å Motta	To Listen	Å Lytte
To Bring	Å Bringe	To Press	Å Trykke
To Work	Å Arbeide	To Promise	Å Love
To Hope	Å Håpe	To Choose	Å Velge
To Live	Å Leve	To Arrive	Å Ankomme
To Find	Å Finne	To Leave	Å dra
To Look	Å Se	To Leave {Something}	Å Forlate
To Search	Å Lete	To Do	Å Gjøre
To See	Å Se	To Order	Å Bestille
To Read	Å Lese	To Pretend	Å late som
To Write	Å Skrive	To Change	Å Forandre
To Learn	Å Lære	I Can	Jeg kan
To Teach	Å Undervise	To Return	Å Returnere
To Take	Å Ta	To Borrow	Å Låne
To Turn on	Å Skru på	To Sit	Å Sitte
To Turn off	Å Skru av	To Need	Å Trenge
To Close	Å Stenge	To Say	Å Si
To Put	Å Anbringe	To Remove	Å Fjerne
To Allow	Å Tillate	To Travel	Å Reise
To Lift	Å Løfte	To Eat	Å Ete, å spise
To Open	Å Åpne	To Exchange	Å Bytte, å veksle
To Wish	Å Ønske	To Mix	Å Blande
To Enter	Å Gå inn	To Belong	Å Høre til
To Come	Å Komme	To Feel	Å Føle
To Move	Å Flytte	To Stop	Å Stanse
To Rent	Å Leie	To Ask	Å Spørre
To Remember	Å Huske	To Answer	Å Svare
To Check	Å Sjekke	To Decide	Å Bestemme
To Call	Å Kalle	To Sell	Å Selge
To Resemble	Å Likne	To Wait	Å Vente

Building Bridges

I Can	Jeg kan
I Do	Jeg Gjør
I Go	Jeg Drar
I Need	Jeg Trenger
I Want	Jeg Vil ha
I See	Jeg Ser
I Like	Jeg Liker
I Say	Jeg Sier
I Talk	Jeg Snakker

Rules:

The infinitive mark "to" is "å" in Norwegian. All of the infinitives above need "å" before them.

Phrases:

Snakker {speak} **du** {you} **norsk** {Norwegian}**?**
Do you speak Norwegian?

Jeg {I} **snakker** {speak} **ikke** {don't} **engelsk** {English}.
I don't speak English.

Hva {what} **sa** {say} **du** {you}?
What did you say?

Reading

Æ or æ– are a ligature between the two words "a" and "e". For example archæology, which is pronounced archeology

Ø or ø - is pronounced as "ir" or "ur" (like "sir")

Å or å - is an "A" with a ring to it, difficult to pronounce in English (like talk orwalk in British English).

For the Norwegian language; grammar, pronunciation, accent, conjugation, reading, and sentence structure are recommended but not required for non-Shakespearean speakers.

European Languages

Section III: Turkish Languages - Turkish

Turkish

The Turkish language originated in the Ottoman Empire. To this day, Turkish is primarily spoken in the countries that were once under Ottoman rule, like Romania, Yugoslavia and Bulgaria, although there are a number of Turkish speakers in Germany. Turkish is spoken in over 35 countries. Turkish is also the official language of Turkey, as the vast majority of its citizens speak the language as a native tongue. What is unique about Turkish is that is has no specific gender connotations, as the same form of a word is used for both male and female.

Spoken in: Turkey, Cyprus

I	Ben
Me	Ben
My	Benim
Mine	Benim
His	Onun
Him	Ona
Her	Onun
Hers	Onun
He	O
She	O
Us	Biz
Our	Bizim
With you	Seninle
With You {Plural}	Seninle
With her	Onunla
With him	Onunla
With Them	Onlarla
Without me	
Without	Siz, siz
Without you	Sensiz
Without you {Plural)	Onlarsiz
Them	Onlar
Their	Onlarin
You	Sen
You {Plural}	Siz
I am	Ben
I was	Ben kediydim.
I will	Ben gidecegim
Are you	Senmi
They	Onlar
Without her	Onsuz
Without Them	Onlarsiz
Without Him	Onsuz
With me	Benimle
For you	Senin icin
To be	Olmak
Yours	Seninki
We are	Biz olmayız
With us	Bizle
Without us	Bizi
Who	Kim

What	Ne	Something	Birşey
If	Eger	Sometimes	Bazen
Similar	Ayni	Somewhere	Baziyerde
Where	Nerede	Yes	Evet
Were	Onlar burdaydilar	No	Hayir
When	Ne zaman	Less	Daha azı.
Only	Sadece	Instead	Onun yerinde
Was	Burdaydim	Including	Dail
Other	Diğeri	While	Bu arada
Since	Den beri	Someone	Biri
Same	Ayni	Again	Tekrar
With	Ile	Away	Uzakda
Already	Cokdan	But	Fakat
Together	Birlikde	Don't	Yapma
Then	Sonra	Both	Ikiside
Than	Den, dan	Because	Cunku
More	Daha	Still, Yet	Hala
Very	Çok	Time	Kac kere
Much, a lot	Çok	Time	Zaman
From	Den	Time	Saat
And	Ve	Also, Too	De ,da
Before	Önce	Around	Etrafinda
After	Sonra	Never	Hic bir zaman
Afterwards	Sonra	Of course	Elbetde
To	E ,a	Here	Burada
The		This	Bu
That	Bu ,	OK	Tamam
That	Bunu	Just	Tam
Is		Although	Halde
Which	Hangi	Through	Ya, ye
For	Icin	It is	Bu
Of		Everywhere	Heryerde
Against	Karsi	Ready	Hazir
Always	Daima	Soon	Yakin
Until	Simdiye kadar	Except	Disimda
Everything	Butun, Herşey	Between	Arasinda
Every	Her	Now	Şimdi.
Even If	Bile	Later	Sonra
Things	Sey ,seyler	Toward	E, a
There	Orada	How Much & How Many	Ne kadar
Into	E dogru, eve dogru, arabaya dogru	Neither	
Or	Yada	None	Hiçbirisi
On	Ustunde	Nobody	Hiçkimse
About	Hakkinda	Maybe	Belki
How	Nasil	Way	Yol
In	Icinde	Why	Neden
Nothing	Hiçbirşey	Side	Yan
At	De, da	Everybody	Herkez
Almost	Neredeyse	A Few	Biraz

Small	Küçük	Name	Isim, ad
Big	Büyük	Last name	Soyat
Hot	Sicak	What is your name	Adin ne?, ismin ne?
Cold	Soğuk.	How old are you	Kac yasindasin?
Up	Yukari	Welcome	Hosgeldin
Down	Aşağı	Years	Yil
Person	Kişi.	Sky	Gök
People	Insanlar	Night	Gece
Fast	Hizli	Light	Isik
Slow	Yavaşla	Darkness	Karanlik
Day	Gün	Morning	Sabah
Tomorrow	Yarin	House	Ev
Today	Bugün	Car	Araba
Yesterday	Dün	Left	Sol
Good	Iyi	Right	Sag
Bad	Kötü	Place	Yer
Hello	Merhaba	Straight	Duz
Goodbye	Gulegule	Parents	Aile
How are you	Nasilsin?	Book	Kitap
Nice to meet you	Seninle tanistigima sevindim	Problem	Problem
Good Night	Iyi geceler	Behind	Arka
Good Afternoon	Iyi öğleden	In-Front	On
Good Morning	Gunaydin	Close	Yakin
Friend	Arkadaş	Far	Uzak
Mom	Anne	Sun	Güneş
Dad	Baba	Better	Daha iyi
Brother	Erkek kardeş	Worse	Daha kötüce
Sister	Kızkardeş	Beautiful	Güzel
Cousin	Kuzen	Real	Gerçek
Grandfather	Büyük baba	Easy	Kolay
Grandmother	Büyük anne	Hard	Sert
Please	Lutfen	Next	Yanimda
Thank you	Tesekkurler	One	Bir
Sorry	Ozurdilerim	Two	Iki
New	Yeni	Three	Üç
Inside	Içinde	Four	Dort
Outside	Dişinda	Five	Beş
Different	Farkli	Six	Alti
First	Ilk	Seven	Yedi
Last	Sonra	Eight	Sekiz
Child	Çocuk	Nine	Dokuz
Man	Erkek	Ten	On
Women	Kadin	Number	Sayı
Week	Hafta	Month	Ay

To Talk	Konuşmak	**To Drive**	Sürmek.
To Walk	Yürümek	**To Pay**	Ödemek.
To Run	Koşmak	**To Buy**	Almak
To Sleep	Uyumak	**To Practice**	Pratik etmek
To Begin	Başlamak	**To Prepare**	Hazirlanmak
To Finish	Bitirmek	**To Meet**	Karsilamak
To Drink	Içmek	**To Fly**	Uçmak.
To Smoke	Içmek	**To Visit**	Ziyaret etmek
To Prefer	Terci etmek	**To Swim**	Yüzmek
To Loose	Kaybetmek	**To Show**	Göstermek
To Forget	Unutmak	**To Know**	Bilmek
To Hold	Tutmak	**To Think**	Düşünmek
To Follow	Takip etmek	**To Believe**	Inanmak
To Continue	Devam etmek	**To Love**	Sevmek
To Want	Istemek	**To Like**	Sevmek
To Stay	Kalmak	**To Use**	Kullanmak
To Keep	Tutmak	**To Try**	Denemek
To Play	Oynamak	**To Understand**	Anlamak
To Get		**To Have**	Saip olmak
To Help	Yardim etmek	**To Happen**	Olmak
To Go	Gitmek	**To Recognize**	Tanimak
To Give	Vermek	**To Hear**	Duymak
To Receive	Almak	**To Listen**	Dinlemek
To Bring	Getirmek	**To Press**	
To Work	Çalışmak	**To Promise**	Söz vermek
To Hope	Umut etmek	**To Choose**	Seçmek
To Live	Yaşamak	**To Arrive**	Varmak
To Find	Bulmak	**To Leave**	Ayrilmak
To Look	Bakmak	**To Leave {Something}**	Birakmak
To Search	Aramak	**To Do**	Yapmak
To See	Görmek	**To Order**	Ismarlamak
To Read	Okumak	**To Pretend**	Gibi yapmak
To Write	Yazmak	**To Change**	Değiştirmek
To Learn	Öğrenmek	**To Be Able To**	Yapabilmek
To Teach	Öğrenmek	**To Return**	Donmek
To Take	Almak	**To Borrow**	Odunc almak
To Turn on	Acmak	**To Sit**	Oturmak
To Turn off	Kapatmak	**To Need**	Ihtiyac duymak
To Close	Kapatmak	**To Say**	Soylemek
To Put	Koymak	**To Remove**	Kimildatmak
To Allow	Izin vermek	**To Travel**	Seyahat etmek
To Lift	Kaldirmak	**To Eat**	Yemek
To Open	Açılmak.	**To Exchange**	Degistirmek
To Wish	Dilemek	**To Mix**	Karistirmak
To Enter	Girmek	**To Belong**	Saip olmak
To Come	Gelmek	**To Feel**	Hissetmek
To Move	Itmek	**To Stop**	Durmak
To Rent	Kiralanmak	**To Ask**	Sormak
To Remember	Hatirlamak	**To Answer**	Cevap vermek
To Check	Kontrol etmek	**To Decide**	Karar verme
To Call	Aramak	**To Sell**	Satmak
To Resemble	Benzemek, sen bana benciyorsun	**To Wait**	Beklemek, bekle

Building Bridges

I Can	Ben Khans
I Do	Ben Yapma
I Go	Ben Gitme
I Need	Ben İhtiyaçlar
I Want	Ben İsteme
I See	Ben Görürüm
I Like	Ben Sevme
I Say	Ben Söyleme
I Talk	Ben Konuşurum

In a sentence with verbs, the second verb goes first, and then the conjugated verb
Example: **I want to go**
ben {I} gitmek {to go} istiyorum {I want - conjugated}

Adjective goes before noun
Example: **good people** – iyi {people} insanlar {good}

Icine dogru, magaranin icine dogru Evin icine

Verb also goes before noun in the sentence
Examples:
I want – Istiyorum
Example: {elma [apple] istiyorum [I want]} – I want an apple
I need – ihtiyacim var
Example: {tuvalete [toilet] ihtiyacim var [I need]} – I need the toilet
I say – soyluyorum
Example: {sana [to you] soyluyorum [I say]} – I say to you
I Like - hoslaniyorum
Example: {Senden [you] hoslaniyorum [I like]}- I like you,
{bundan [this] hoslaniyorum [I like]}- I like this
I go - gidiyorum
Example: {eve [home] gidiyorum [I go]} - I am going home

A - a; For example: **U**nder
C - ce; For example: **J**enny
Ç – çe; For example: **Ch**ance
Ğ – ğe
İ - i; For example: **I**nside
Ö - ö; For example: **Tu**rn
Ş - şe; For example: **Sh**all
U - u; For example: **Moo**d
Ü - ü: For example: **Mu**ndial

For the Turkish language; grammar, pronunciation, accent, conjugation, reading, and sentence structure are recommended but not required for non-Shakespearean speakers.

73

European Languages

Section IV: Slavic Languages
- Polish
- Russian

Polish

The official language of Poland is Polish. About 97 percent of Poland's citizens declare Polish as their native tongue, which is a very high amount of Poles that speak the language. At one point Polish was more widespread than it is now, as Russia has overcame the language in popularity in surrounding areas like Lithuania and Ukraine. However, Polish wasn't totally wiped out, that is, many people still know the language but don't speak it as frequently. German has greatly influenced the vocabulary of Polish, as Germany borders Poland. However, Germany isn't the only influential language. Belaruse, Russia the Czech Republic and Slovakia all have had their fair share in influencing Polish as well.

Spoken in: Poland

I	Ja
Me	Mnie
My	Mój
Mine	Mój
His	Jego
Him	Jego
Her	Jej
Hers	Jej
He	On
She	Ona
Us	Nam
Our	Nasz
With you	Z tobą
With You {Plural}	Z nami
With her	Z nią
With him	Z nim
With Them	Z nimi
Without me	Beze mnie
Without	Bez
Without you	Bez ciebie
Without you {Plural}	Bez was
Them, They	Ich, Oni *(male)*/ One *(female)*
Their	Ich
You	Ty
You {Plural}	Wy
I am	Ja jestem
I was	Ja byłem
I will	Ja będę
Are you	Czy jesteś
We	My
Without her	Bez niej
Without Them	Bez nich
Without Him	Bez niego
With me	Beze mnie
For you	Dla Ciebie
To be	Być
Yours	Twój
We are	My jesteśmy
With us	Z nami
Without us	Bez nas
Who	Kto

What	Co	Something	Coś
If	Jeżeli	Sometimes	Czasami
Similar	Podobny	Somewhere	Gdzieś
Where	Gdzie	Yes	Tak
Were	Był (you, he) Była (she) Było (it)	No	Nie
When	Kiedy	Less	Mniej
Only	Tylko	Instead	Zamiast
Was	(m)Byłem/(f)Byłam	Including	Zawierać
Other	Inny	While	Kiedy *(part.)*, Chwila*(n)*
Since	Od	Someone	Ktoś
Same	Trochę	Again	Znów
With	Z	Away	Daleko
Already	Już	But	Ale
Together	Razem	Don't	Nie
Then	Potem	Both	Obydwa
Than	Niż	Because	Ponieważ
More	Więcej	Still, Yet	Nadal, Jednak *(part.)* OR Jeszcze *(adv.)*
Very	Bardzo	Time	Raz
Much, a lot	Dużo	Time	Czas
From	Od	Time	Godzina
And	I	Also, Too	Również
Before	Przed	Around	Wokół
After	Po	Never	Nigdy
Afterwards	Potem	Of Course	Oczywiście
To	Do	Here	Tutaj
The	Ten (m)/ Ta(f) To (neutral)	This	Ten (m)/ Ta (f) To(neutral)
That	To	OK	W porządku
That	Że	Just	Tylko
Is	Jest	Although	Chociaż
Which	Który	Through	Przez
For	Dla	It is	To jest
Of	Z	Everywhere	Wszędzie
Against	Przeciw	Ready	Gotowe
Always	Zawsze	Soon	Wkrótce
Until	Do	Except	Oprócz
Everything	Wszystko	Between	Pomiędzy
Every	Każdy	Now	Teraz
Even If	Nawet, jeżeli	Later	Później
Things	Rzeczy	Toward	W kierunku
There	Tam	How Much/many	Ile
Into	Do	Neither	Żaden
Or	Lub	None	Nic *OR* Żaden
On	Na	Nobody	Nikt
About	O	Maybe	Może
How	Jak	Way	Droga *(route)* OR Sposób *(method)*
In	W	Why	Dlaczego
Nothing	Nic	Side	Strona
At	W	Everybody	Wszyscy
Almost	Prawie	A Few	Kilka

Small	Mały	Name	Imię
Big	Duży	Last name	Nazwisko
Hot	Gorący	What is your name	Jak masz na imię
Cold	Zimny	How old are you	Ile masz lat
Up	W górę	Welcome	Witamy
Down	W dół	Years	Lata
Person	Osoba	Sky	Niebo
People	Ludzie	Night	Noc
Fast	Szybko	Light	Światło
Slow	Wolno	Darkness	Ciemność
Day	Dzień	Morning	Ranek
Tomorrow	Jutro	House	Dom
Today	Dzisiaj	Car	Samochód
Yesterday	Wczoraj	Left	Lewy (-a) (f)
Good	Dobry	Right	Prawy (-a) (f)
Bad	Zły	Place	Miejsce
Hello	Cześć, halo	Straight	Prosto
Goodbye	Do widzenia	Parents	Rodzice
How are you	Jak się masz	Book	Książka
Nice to meet you	Miło mi poznać	Problem	Problem
Good Night	Dobranoc	Behind	Z tyłu
Good Afternoon	Dzień dobry	Front	Z przodu
Good Morning	Dzień dobry	Near	Niedaleko
Friend	Przyjaciel (m) / Przyjaciółka (f)	Far	Daleko
Mom	Mama	Sun	Słońce
Dad	Tata	Better	Lepiej
Brother	Brat	Worse	Gorzej
Sister	Siostra	Beautiful	Piękny
Cousin	Kuzyn (m) /Kuzynka (f)	Real	Prawdziwy
Grandfather	Dziadek	Easy	Łatwy
Grandmother	Babcia	Hard	Trudny, OR Twardy
Please	Proszę	Next	Następny
Thank you	Dziękuję	One	Jeden
Sorry	Przepraszam	Two	Dwa
New	Nowy	Three	Trzy
Inside	Wewnątrz	Four	Cztery
Outside	Na zewnątrz	Five	Pięć
Different	Różny	Six	Sześć
First	Pierwszy	Seven	Siedem
Last	Ostatni	Eight	Osiem
Child	Dziecko	Nine	Dziewięć
Man	Mężczyzna	Ten	Dziesięć
Women	Kobieta	Number	Numer
Week	Tydzień	Month	Miesiąc

To Talk	Rozmawiać	**To Drive**	Jechać
To Walk	Spacerować	**To Pay**	Płacić
To Run	Biegać	**To Buy**	Kupować
To Sleep	Spać	**To Practice**	Ćwiczyć
To Begin	Rozpocząć	**To Prepare**	Przygotować
To Finish	Skończyć	**To Meet**	Spotkać
To Drink	Pić	**To Fly**	Lecieć
To Smoke	Palić	**To Visit**	Odwiedzać
To Prefer	Woleć	**To Swim**	Pływać
To Lose	Zgubić	**To Show**	Pokazywać
To Forget	Zapomnieć	**To Know**	Wiedzieć
To Hold	Trzymać	**To Think**	Myśleć
To Follow	Stosować	**To Believe**	Wierzyć
To Continue	Kontynuować	**To Love**	Kochać
To Want	Chcieć	**To Like**	Lubić
To Stay	Przebywać	**To Use**	Używać
To Keep	Trzymać	**To Try**	Próbować
To Play	Grać	**To Understand**	Rozumieć
To Get	Dostać	**To Have**	Mieć
To Help	Pomóc	**To Happen**	Zdarzyć
To Go	Iść	**To Recognize**	Rozpoznać
To Give	Dać	**To Hear**	Słyszeć
To Receive	Otrzymać	**To Listen**	Słuchać
To Bring	Przynieść	**To Press**	Przyciskać
To Work	Pracować	**To Promise**	Obiecać
To Hope	Mieć nadzieję	**To Choose**	Wybrać
To Live	Mieszkać	**To Arrive**	Przyjechać
To Find	Znaleźć	**To Leave**	Wyjechać
To Look	Wyglądać	**To Leave {Something}**	Zostawić
To Search	Szukać	**To Do**	Robić
To See	Widzieć	**To Order**	Zamówić
To Read	Czytać	**To Pretend**	Udawać
To Write	Pisać	**To Change**	Zmienić
To Learn	Uczyć się	**I Can**	Ja mogę
To Teach	Uczyć	**To Return**	Wrócić
To Take	Brać	**To Borrow**	Pożyczyć
To Turn on	Włączyć	**To Sit**	Siedzieć
To Turn off	Wyłączyć	**To Need**	Potrzebować
To Close	Zamknąć	**To Say**	Powiedzieć
To Put	Położyć	**To Remove**	Usunąć
To Allow	Pozwolić	**To Travel**	Podróżować
To Lift	Podnieść	**To Eat**	Jeść
To Open	Otworzyć	**To Exchange**	Wymienić
To Wish	Życzyć	**To Mix**	Mieszać
To Enter	Wejść	**To Belong**	Należeć
To Come	Przybyć	**To Feel**	Czuć
To Move	Ruszać	**To Stop**	Zatrzymać
To Rent	Wypożyczyć, wynająć	**To Ask**	Zapytać
To Remember	Pamiętać	**To Answer**	Odpowiedzieć
To Check	Sprawdzać	**To Decide**	Zdecydować
To Call	Dzwonić	**To Sell**	Sprzedawać
To Resemble	Być podobnym	**To Wait**	Czekać

Building Bridges

I Can	(Ja) mogę
I Do	Ja robię
I Go	Ja idę
I Need	Ja potrzebuję
I Want	Ja chcę
I See	Ja widzę
I Like	Ja lubię
I Say	Ja mówię
I Talk	Ja rozmawiam

Translator's Note: In the last table, "Ja" is usually omitted"

I go there
Ja idę tam
Ja (I) idę (go) tam
(there)

I can't live with her
Nie mogę z nią
Nie (No) mogę (I can) z (with) nią (her)

I don't want to talk with them now
Nie chcę z nimi rozmawiać Teraz
Nie (no) chcę (I want) z (with) nimi (them) rozmawiać (to talk) teraz (now)

Ą – on

Ć – ch

Ę – en

Ł - ehw

Ń - ni

Ó - oo

Ś - sh

Ź - s

Ź - s

For the Polish language; grammar, pronunciation, accent, conjugation, reading, and sentence structure are recommended but not required for non-Shakespearean speakers.

Russian

As many Russian words have Bulgarian roots, Russian is the most common language in Europe and Russia. Perhaps a reason for its popularity is because it also derives vocabulary and connotations from the languages of French, English, German, Latin and Greek. It is also one of the official languages of United Nations. After the Soviet Union fell apart, Russian was only the official language of present day Russia, and other countries that were part of the Union were encouraged to speak their native tongue. Prior, all countries that were part of the Union were required to speak only Russian, though it still remains the official language of Ukraine, Kazakhstan, Kyrgyzstan and Belarus. However, Russian is not only limited to Europe, as it is the tenth most spoken language in the United States and spoken by approximately 750,000 people in Israel.

Spoken in: Russia, former Soviet republics

I	Ya
Me	Meene
My	Moi
Mine	Moi
His	Yivo
Him	Oun
Her	Anna
Hers	Yeo
He	Oun
She	Ona
Us	Oni
Our	Nashe
With you	S Toboi
With You {Plural}	S Vami
With her	S Nei
With him	S Nim
With Them	S Nimi
Without me	Bez mena
Without	Bez
Without you	Bez tebya
Without you {Plural}	Bez vas
Them, They	Oni
Their	Ih
You	Ti
You {Plural}	Vi
I am	Ya
I was	Ya bil
I will	Ya budu
Are you	Vi
We	Mey
Without her	Bez neyo
Without Them	Bez nih
Without Him	Bez nego
With me	Bez menya
For you	Dlya Tebya
To be	Bit'
Yours	Tviou
We are	Me
With us	S nami
Without us	Bez nas
Who	Ktou

What	Chto	**Something**	Chto to
If	Esli	**Sometimes**	Inogda
Similar	Pohozhiy	**Somewhere**	Gde to
Where	Gde	**Yes**	Da
Were	Bili	**No**	Net
When	Kogda	**Less**	Menche
Only	Tolka	**Instead**	Vmesto
Was	Bil	**Including**	Vkluchit'
Other	Drugoe	**While**	Poka
Since	S teh por	**Someone**	Kto to
Same as	Takie zhe kak	**Again**	Opyat'
With	S	**Away**	Ot
Already	Uzhe	**But**	No
Together	Vmeste	**Don't**	Ne
Then	Posle tavo	**Both**	Oba
Than	Chem	**Because**	Potomu chto
More	Bol'she	**Still, Yet**	Do sih por
Very	Ochen'	**Time**	Ras
Much, a lot	Mnogo	**Time**	Vremya
From	Ot	**Time**	Vremya
And	E	**Also, Too**	Takzhe
Before	Ranshe	**Around**	Vokrug
After	Posle	**Never**	Nikogda
Afterwards	Potom	**Of Course**	Konechno
To	K	**Here**	Zdes'
The		**This**	Etot
That	Etta	**OK**	Horosho
That	To	**Just**	Tol'ko
Is	Est'	**Although**	Hotya
Which	Kakoi	**Through**	Naskvoz'
For	Dlya	**It is**	On est'
Of		**Everywhere**	Vezde
Against	Protiv	**Ready**	Gotov
Always	Vsegda	**Soon**	Skoro
Until	Do	**Except**	Za isklucheniem
Everything	Vse	**Between**	Mezhdu
Every	Kazhdiy	**Now**	Teper'
Even If	Esli dazhe	**Later**	Pozzhe
Things	Vesh	**Toward**	K
There	Tam	**How Much & How Many**	Skolka Stoyit Skolka
Into	Vstuplenie	**Neither**	Ni te
Or	Ili	**None**	Nikakie
On	Na	**Nobody**	Nikto
About	O	**Maybe**	Mozhet bit'
How	Kak	**Way**	Put'
In	V	**Why**	Pochemu
Nothing	Nechevo	**Side**	Bock
At	Va	**Everybody**	Vse Vemesti
Almost	Pachti	**A Few**	Neskol'ko

Small	Malenkii	**Name**	Imya
Big	Bol'shoi	**Last name**	Familiya
Hot	Goryachii	**What is your name**	Kak tebya zovut?
Cold	Holodnii	**How old are you**	Skol'ko tebe let?
Up	Vverh	**Welcome**	Dobro Pozhalovat'
Down	Vniz	**Years**	Goda
Person	Chelovek	**Sky**	Neba
People	Ludi	**Night**	Noch
Fast	Bistrii	**Light**	Svet
Slow	Medlenii	**Darkness**	Temnota
Day	Den'	**Morning**	Utro
Tomorrow	Zavtra	**House**	Dom
Today	Segodnya	**Car**	Mashina
Yesterday	Vchera	**Left**	Levo
Good	Horosho	**Right**	Pravo
Bad	Ploho	**Place**	Mesto
Hello	Zdravstvuiite	**Straight**	Pryamo
Goodbye	Dosvidaniya	**Parents**	Roditeli
How are you	Kak vi	**Book**	Kniga
Nice to meet you	Rad Poznakomitsya Or Ochin Preatna	**Problem**	Problema
Good Night	Dobroii Nochi	**Behind**	Szadi
Good Afternoon	Dobrii Den'	**Front**	Pered
Good Morning	Dobroe Utro	**Close**	Ryadom
Friend	Droog	**Far**	Daleko
Mom	Mama	**Sun**	Solnce
Dad	Papa	**Better**	Luchshe
Brother	Brat	**Worse**	Ploho
Sister	Sestra	**Beautiful**	Krasivii
Cousin	Kuzen	**Real**	Nastoyashii
Grandfather	Dedushka	**Easy**	Legkii
Grandmother	Babushka	**Hard**	Tyazhelii
Please	Pozhaluiista	**Next**	Sleduushii
Thank you	Spasibo	**One**	Odin
Sorry	Izvinite	**Two**	Dva
New	Novae	**Three**	Tri
Inside	Vnutri	**Four**	Chetire
Outside	Snaruzhi	**Five**	Pyat'
Different	Drugoii	**Six**	Shest'
First	Pervii	**Seven**	Sem'
Last	Poslednii	**Eight**	Vosem'
Child	Rebenok	**Nine**	Devyat'
Man	Chelovek	**Ten**	Desyat'
Women	Zhenshina	**Number**	Noumer
Week	Nidela	**Month**	Mesits

To Talk	Gavaritzz	**To Drive**	Yezditz
To Walk	Haditzz	**To Pay**	Platitz
To Run	Begitzz	**To Buy**	Pacoopatz
To Sleep	Spaitzz	**To Practice**	Practicavatza
To Begin	Nachinatz	**To Prepare**	Pregatavlatsa
To Finish	Conchatz	**To Meet**	Vstrechatsa
To Drink	Peetz	**To Fly**	Leetatz
To Smoke	Cooritz	**To Visit**	
To Prefer	Pretpachitatz	**To Swim**	Plavitz
To Loose	Tiratz	**To Show**	Pakazatz
To Forget	Zabivatz	**To Know**	Znatz
To Hold	Deerjatz	**To Think**	Doomitz
To Follow	Sledavitz	**To Believe**	Veritz
To Continue	Pradaljatz	**To Love**	Lubitz
To Want	Hatetz	**To Like**	Nravitzsa
To Stay	Astatsa	**To Use**	Espolzivits
To Keep	Derjatz	**To Try**	Probavitz
To Play	Eagratz	**To Understand**	Panematz
To Get	Dostatz	**To Have**	Eemetz
To Help	Pamagatz	**To Happen**	Sloochitsa
To Go	Eetsee	**To Recognize**	Ooznavats
To Give	Otdavatz	**To Hear**	Slishits
To Receive	Palochatz	**To Listen**	Slooshits
To Bring	Prenasitz	**To Press**	Pressavatz
To Work	Rabotitz	**To Promise**	Abeshatz
To Hope	Nadaeitsa	**To Choose**	Vebiratz
To Live	Jitz	**To Arrive**	Preyijatz
To Find	Nitze	**To Leave**	Ooyijatz
To Look	Smatretz	**To Leave {Something}**	Ostavits
To Search	Eeskatz	**To Do**	Delitz
To See	Veeditz	**To Order**	Zakazatz
To Read	Cheetatz	**To Pretend**	Pretendavatz
To Write	Peesatz	**To Change**	Pamynatz
To Learn	Oocheetza	**I Can**	Ya Magoo
To Teach	Oocheetz	**To Return**	Vizrashatz
To Take	Vzatz	**To Borrow**	Zanymatz
To Turn on	Vkloocheetz	**To Sit**	Seedetz
To Turn off	Vickloochitz	**To Need**	Noojna
To Close	Zatkrits	**To Say**	Skazatz
To Put	Palajitz	**To Remove**	Oobratz
To Allow	Rajrishitz	**To Travel**	Pooteshestvavtz
To Lift	Padnatz	**To Eat**	Cooshitz
To Open	Otkritz	**To Exchange**	Pomynatz
To Wish	Jilatz	**To Mix**	Mishatz
To Enter	Viyte	**To Belong**	Prenadlijatz
To Come	Preetze	**To Feel**	Choostvivtz
To Move	Peredvigatza	**To Stop**	Ostanavitza
To Rent	Rentavatz	**To Ask**	Spraseetz
To Remember	Zapomynatz	**To Answer**	Otvetitz
To Check	Praviratz	**To Decide**	Reeshitz
To Call	Pazvatz	**To Sell**	Pradatz
To Resemble	Pahoja	**To Wait**	Zjdatz

Building Bridges:

I Can	Ya magoo
I Do	Ya deliu
I Go	Ya pashol
I Need	Mene nada
I Want	Ya Hachoo
I See	Ya veejoo
I Like	Mene nravitsa
I Say	Ya gavaroo
I Talk	Ya gavaroo

Phrases:

Thank you, what did you say

Spasibo, chto vy skazAli?

Spasibo {Thank you}, chto {what} vy {you} skazAli {say}?

What are you doing tomorrow?

Ti Zavtra chto dalizz?

Ti {you} Zavtra {tomorrow} chto {what} dalizz {doing}?

Do you understand me

Vi menya Panematz?

Vi {you} menya {me} Panematz {understand}?

For the Russian language; grammar, pronunciation, accent, conjugation, and sentence structure are recommended but not required for non-Shakespeare speakers.

Chapter 2: Afro Asiatic Languages

Section I: Semitic Languages – Hebrew

Hebrew

Hebrew is an ancient language with a rich cultural history. Commonly associated with Judaism, the language has strong ties to the religion and the Jewish way of life. In fact, Jews are often referred to as Hebrews, though this term is much more common when referring too ancient Jews as opposed to modern ones. Much of the language's rich history can be found in the many ancient Jewish texts that Hebrew is used in such as the Torah and many other historic texts. The word Hebrew means "to cross over," which originated from the Semitic people crossing the Euphrates River.

Spoken in: Israel

I	Ani
Me	Ani
My	Sheli
Mine	Sheli
His	Shelo
Him	Whoo
Her	Hee
Hers	Shela
He	Whoo
She	Hee
Us	Anakhnu
Our	Shelanu
With you	Itkha
With You {Plural}	Itkhem
With her	Itah
With him	Ito
With Them	Itam
Without me	Biladi
Without	Bli
Without you	Biladekha
Without you {Plural}	Biladkhem
Them, They	Hem
Their	Shelahaem
You	Ata
You {Plural}	Itkhem
I am	Ani
I was	Ahiiti
I will	Ani hyhae
Are you	Atta?
We	Anakhno
Without her	Biladaeha
Without Them	Biladam
Without Him	Biladav
With me	Iiti
For you	Bishvilkha
To be	Lihiot
Your, yours	Shelkha
We are	Anakhnu
With us	Itanu
Without us	Biladainu
Who	Mi

What	Maa	**Something**	Mashaeho
If	Iim	**Sometimes**	Lefamim
Similar	Cmo	**Somewhere**	Aifo shaeho
Where	Aifo	**Yes**	Ken
Were	Aiiho	**No**	Lo
When	Mataai	**Less**	Pakhot
Only	Raak	**Instead**	Bimkom
Was	Hayaa	**Including**	Kolel
Other	Akher	**While**	Bentaim
Since	Maehaz	**Someone**	Mishaehoo
Same	Cmo	**Again**	Hod paam, shoov
With	Iim	**Away**	Rakhok
Already	Kvar	**But**	Aval
Together	Behyaahad	**Don't**	Al
Then	Az	**Both**	Shnaihem
Than	Mi	**Because**	Biglal
More	Yoter	**Still, Yet**	Hod
Very	Mehod	**Time**	Pahamim
Much, a lot	Arbeh	**Time**	Zmaan
From	Mi	**Time**	Shaha
And	Ve	**Also, Too**	Gaam
Before	Lifnei	**Around**	Misaviv
After	Akharai	**Never**	Leholam, af paham
Afterwards	Akharkaakh	**Of course**	Betakh
To	Le	**Here**	Po
The	Haa	**This**	Ze
That	Ze	**OK**	Beseder
That	Shae	**Just**	Kvar
Is	Ze	**Although**	Bekholzot
Which	Azea	**Through**	Derekh
For	Bishvil	**It is**	Ze
Of	Shel	**Everywhere**	Bekol makom
Against	Neged	**Ready**	Mokhaan
Always	Tamid	**Soon**	Kvar
Until	Haad	**Except**	Khotz
Everything	Akkol	**Between**	Bin
Every	Kol	**Now**	Akhshav
Even If	Afilu	**Later**	Akharkaakh
Thing{s}	Dvarim	**Toward**	Likraat
There	Shaam	**How Much & How Many**	Kama
Into	Letokh	**Neither**	Gaam lo
Or	Ho	**None**	Kloom
On	Al	**Nobody**	Af aikhad
About	Al	**Maybe**	Oolay
How	Aiikh	**Way**	Derekh
In	Bae	**Why**	Lama
Nothing	Kluum	**Side**	Tzadd
At	Bae	**Everybody**	Kulam
Almost	Kimat	**A Few**	Kama

Small	Kataan	Name	Shem
Big	Gadol	Last name	Shem mishpakha
Hot	Kham	What is you name	Ma shimca
Cold	Kaar	How old are you	Ben kaama atta
Up	Lemalah	Welcome	Brokhim habahim
Down	Lematah	Years	Shannim
Person	Bin hadaam	Sky	Shamaiim
People	Anashim	Night	Laila
Fast	Maaher	Light	Hor
Slow	Lehaat	Darkness	Khoshekh
Day	Yom	Morning	Boker
Tomorrow	Makhar	House	Baaiit
Today	Hayoom	Car	Aoto, mikhonit
Yesterday	Etmol	Left	Smola
Good	Tov	Right	Yamina
Bad	Raah	Place	Makom
Hello	Shalom	Straight	Yashar
Goodbye	Lehitrahahot	Parents	Horim
How are you	Mashlomkha	Book	Sefer
Nice to meet you	Nahaim mehod	Problem	Bahaya
Good Night	Lila tov	Behind	Mae-hakhorai
Good Afternoon	Tzoorahim tovim	Front	Lifnei
Good Morning	Boker tov	Near	Karov
Friend	Khaver	Far	Rakhok
Mom	Imma	Sun	Shemesh
Dad	Abba	Better	Yoter Tov
Brother	Akh	Worse	Garooha
Sister	Akhot	Beautiful	Yafaeh
Cousin	Ben dod	Real	Hamiti
Grandfather	Saaba	Easy	Kal
Grandmother	Safta	Hard	Kashae
Please	Bevakasha	Next	Habaah
Thank you	Toda	One	Aikhad
Sorry	Mitztaeher	Two	Shtaaim
New	Khadash	Three	Shalosh
Inside	Befnim	Four	Harbah
Outside	Bakhootz	Five	Khamesh
Different	Akher	Six	Shesh
First	Rishon	Seven	Sheva
Last	Akharon	Eight	Shmonae
Child	Yeled	Nine	Taesha
Man	Iish	Ten	Eser
Woman	Iisha	Number	Mispar
Week	Shavoha	Month	Khodesh

To Talk	Ledaber	**To Drive**	Linhog
To Walk	Lalikhit	**To Pay**	Leshalem
To Run	Larootz	**To Buy**	Liknot
To Sleep	Lishon	**To Practice**	Laehitamen
To Begin	Lahatkhil	**To Prepare**	Laehitkonen
To Finish	Ligmor	**To Meet**	Lifgosh
To Drink	Lishtot	**To Fly**	Laahoof
To Smoke	Laehashan	**To Visit**	Levaker
To Prefer	Lahadif	**To Swim**	Lizkhot
To Loose	Leh-ah-bed	**To Show**	Laharot
To Forget	Lishkoaakh	**To Know**	Ladahat
To Hold	Lahakhzik	**To Think**	Lakhshov
To Follow	Lahakov	**To Believe**	Lahamin
To Continue	Lehamshikh	**To Love**	Lehaehov
To Want	Lirtzot	**To Like**	Lehaehov
To Stay	Laeishaer	**To Use**	Lehishtamesh
To Keep	Lishmor	**To Try**	Lenasot
To Play	Lesakhek	**To Understand**	Laehavin
To Get	Lekabel	**To Have**	Yesh
To Help	Lahazor	**To Happen**	Likrot
To Go	Lalikhit	**To Recognize**	La-hakir
To Give	Lattet	**To Hear**	Lishmoha
To Receive	Lekabel	**To Listen**	Lahakshiv
To Bring	Lahahavii	**To Press**	Lilkhotz
To Work	Lahahvod	**To Promise**	Laehavtiakh
To Hope	Lekavot	**To Choose**	Livkhor
To Live	Likhiot	**To Arrive**	Lahagya
To Find	Limtzo	**To Leave**	Lahazov
To Look	Laehistakel	**To Leave {Something}**	Lahashir
To Search	Lekhapess	**To Do**	Lahasot
To See	Liroot	**To Order**	Lahazmin
To Read	Likro	**To Pretend**	Laeitkhazot
To Write	Likhtov	**To Change**	Lahakhlif
To Learn	Lilmod	**I Can**	Ani Yakhol
To Teach	Lelamed	**To Return**	Lakhzor
To Take	Lakakhat	**To Borrow**	Lahahalvot
To Turn on	Lahadlik	**To Sit**	Lashevet
To Turn off	Lekhabot	**To Need**	Leitztarekh
To Close	Lisgor	**To Say**	Lomar, lahagid
To Put	Lassim	**To Remove**	Laehotzi
To Allow	Lahaharshot	**To Travel**	Letayel
To Lift	Laharim	**To Eat**	Laehekhol
To Open	Liftoakh	**To Exchange**	Laehakh
To Wish	Laehakhel	**To Mix**	Laeharbev
To Enter	Laeikaness	**To Belong**	Laeihot shaayakh
To Come	La-vo	**To Feel**	Lahargish
To Move	Lahaziz	**To Stop**	Lahafsik, lehatzor
To Rent	Lahazkir	**To Ask**	Levakesh, lishol
To Remember	Lizkor	**To Answer**	Lahaanot
To Check	Livdok	**To Decide**	Lahakhlit
To Call	Lehitkasher	**To Sell**	Limkor
To Resemble	Laehirahot	**To Wait**	Lekhakot

Building Bridges

I Can	Ani Yakhol
I Do	Ani Hosae
I Go	Ani Holekh
I Need	Ani Tzarikh
I Want	Ani Rotzae
I See	Ani Rohae
I Like	Ani Hohaev
I Say	Ani Homer
I Talk	Ani Medaber

Rules:

1- The adjective goes after the noun. For example sunglasses. Mishkafaei {Glasses} Shemesh {Sun}

2- The word "Et" in Hebrew, this is a type of word that goes before the word "the" when talking about a noun, or speaking about a person. For example "You take the book". Atta {you} Tikakh {take} **"Et"** ha{the} Sefer{book}. Or the word "Et" can be also used when describing a person while giving an order. For example "bring Michael". Tavi {bring} **"Et"** Michael.

3- The word "Kh" sounds

4- "Your", "my", "his", etc... will always be after the noun. For example: "Your office - Hamisrad {office} Shelkha{your}"

Phrases:

I want to go home

Ani rotze lalaikhit abayta

Ani {I} rotze {[I]want} lalaikhit {to go} abayta {to the house}

Where are you from?

Mi aifo atta

Mi {from} aifo {where} atta {you are}

I need to read your book

Ani Tzarikh Likro et hasefer shelka

Ani {I} Tzarikh {Need} Likro {to read} et hasefer {book} shelkha {your}

For the Hebrew language; grammar, pronunciation, accent, conjugation, and sentence structure are recommended but not required for non-Shakespearean speakers. For the Hebrew language it's also recommended to learn how to pronounce the "kh" (refer back to introduction).

Afro Asiatic Languages

Section II: Semitic Languages
  - Classical Arabic
  - Lebanese Arabic
  - Syrian Arabic
  - Palestinian
  - Egyptian Arabic
  - Moroccan Arabic
  - Iraqi Arabic
  - Saudi Arabic

Modern Standard Arabic (Classical Arabic)

Modern Standard Arabic (MSA) is a modern form of Classical Arabic written in the Qur'an. The language isn't spoken in a small, social environment, rather, by official means of communication like Arabic television personalities and the media. It is a more official Arabic language; any other version of MSA is considered a dialect (referred to as "colloquial Arabic.") Most people in the Middle East and some parts of Africa speak some version of the language, though under most circumstances are able to use MSA to communicate with each other, despite their varying dialects. Still, MSA is the official language of all Middle Eastern countries. MSA is closely related to the religion of Islam, though many Muslims don't speak the dialect.

The major groups are:
Egyptian Arabic
Maghreb Arabic (Algerian Arabic, Moroccan Arabic, Tunisian Arabic, Maltese and western Libyan)
Levantine Arabic (Western Syrian, Lebanese, Israel, Palestinian, and western Jordanian, Cypriot Maronite Arabic)
Iraqi Arabic (and Khuzestani Arabic) - with significant differences between the more Arabian-like gilit-dialects of the south and the more conservative qeltu-dialects of the northern cities
Gulf Arabic (Eastern Syrian, Kuwaiti, Saudi Arabian, Persian Gulf coast from Iraq to Oman including much of Saudi Arabia's Eastern Province, and minorities on the other side)
Other varieties include:
Massaniya (in Mauritania and western Sahara)
Andalusi Arabic (extinct, but important role in literary history)
Sudanese Arabic (with a dialectcontinuum into Chad)
Baharna Arabic (Bahrain, Saudi Eastern Province, and Oman)
Hijazi Arabic (West Coast of Saudi Arabia, Northern Saudi Arabia, eastern Jordan, Western Iraq)
Najdi Arabic (Najd region of central Saudi Arabia)
Yemeni Arabic (Yemen to southern Saudi Arabia)

Spoken in: Algeria, Bahrain, Egypt, Iraq, Jordan, Kuwait, Lebanon, Libya, Mauritania, Morocco, Oman, Qatar, Saudi Arabia, Sudan, Syria, Tunisia, United Arab Emirates, Palestine (West Bank and Gaza), Western Sahara (SADR), Yemen by a majority, and in many other countries, such as Israel and Iran, as a minority language; it is also the liturgical language of Islam.

I	Ana
Me	Ana
My	Ee
Mine	Lee
His	Hu
Him	Howa
Her	Haa
Hers	Hya
He	Hu
She	Hiya
Us	Nahno
Our	Linaa
With you	Maak
With You {Plural}	Maantum
With her	Maahya
With him	Haahu
With Them	Mahuum
Without me	Bidoonee
Without	Bidoon
Without you	Bidoonaak
Without you {Plural}	Bidoantum
Them	Hum
Their	Hum
You	Anta
We	Nahno
You {Plural}	Antuum
I am	Ana
I was	Ana kont
I will	Ana rah
Are you	Hal inta
They	Hum
Without her	Bidoonhya
Without Them	Bidoonhum
Without Him	Bidoonhu
With me	Maai
For you	Licka
To be	Yakoon
Yours	Ak
We are	Nahnu
With us	Maana
Without us	Bedoonna
Who	Man

What	Maa	Something	Shay maa
If	Aza	Sometimes	Ahyaanan
Similar	Misl	Somewhere	Ayy makaan
Where	Ayn	Yes	Naam
Were	Cam	No	La
When	Matta	Less	Aqal
Only	Fokat	Instead	Wadala Min
Was	Kont	Including	Tashmal
Other	Okhra	While	Fatra
Since	Meta	Someone	Ahad maa
Same	Nafsal	Again	Min jedid
With	Maah	Away	Bayda
Already	Qabl al an	But	Lekan
Together	Maa	Don't	Leaa
Then	Baad althalk, th-hem	Both	Alkala
Than	Min	Because	Imdad
More	Akhtar	Still	Sakin
Very	Jidadan	Time	Mara
Much, a lot	Akhtar	Time	Zemaan
From	Min	Time	Saa
And	Wa	Also, Too	Aydan
Before	Qabl	Around	Hawl
After	Baad	Never	Abadan
Afterwards	Baad dhalik	Of course	Akeed
To	Li	Here	Huna
The	Al	This	Haaza
That	Haaza	OK	Hasnan
That	Likay	Just	Mujarrad
Is	Haaza	Although	Al aragmaa
Which	Ayy	Through	Min khilal
For	Lil	It is	Hya takoon
Of	Min	Everywhere	Kul makan
Against	Ded	Ready	Jaaiz
Always	Daa'iman	Soon	Qariba
Until	Hadaata	Except	Astathan
Everything	Alkulu	Between	Bin
Every	Kul	Now	Al aan
Even If	Hata lou	Later	Tajloz
Things	Aishi	Toward	Aly
There	Hunak	How Much & How Many	Kam
Into	Lil	Neither	Wa la
Or	O	None	Lla shay
On	Ala	Nobody	La ahad
About	Ala	Maybe	Rabmaa
How	Kif	Way	Tareeq
In	Fee	Why	Limaaza
Nothing	Laa shay	Side	Anhaz
At	Fee	Everyone	Kul shakhs
Almost	Anja	A Few	Aleel

Small	Sughair	**Name**	Ism
Big	Kabhir	**Last name**	Esm el alla
Hot	Haar	**What is your name**	Maa Ismaak
Cold	Baarid	**How old are you**	Kam omrac
Up	Raphah	**Welcome**	Marhaban
Down	Adni	**Years**	Saanin
Person	Alshakhs	**Sky**	Samaaha
People	Naas	**Night**	Laila
Fast	Saryah	**Light**	Noor
Slow	Tmaal	**Darkness**	Muzlim
Day	Alyom	**Morning**	Sabah
Tomorrow	Gada	**House**	Baiet
Today	Alyom	**Car**	Sayaara
Yesterday	Ams	**Left**	Yassar
Good	Jid	**Right**	Yameen
Bad	Syaah	**Place**	Mekan
Hello	Marhabah	**Straight**	Ala Tool
Goodbye	Wadaaha	**Parents**	Waaladaya
How are you	Kif halaak	**Book**	Kitaab
Nice to meet you	Tasharafna	**Problem**	Mashekla
Good Night	Tisbah Alkhir	**Behind**	Wara
Good Afternoon	Masa Alkhir	**Front**	Al Amaam
Good Morning	Sabaah alkhir	**Near**	Kareeb
Friend	Sadiik	**Far**	Bahiid
Mom	Um	**Sun**	Shams
Dad	Ab	**Better**	Afdal
Brother	Akh	**Worse**	Aswa
Sister	Akhta	**Beautiful**	Jammil
Cousin	abnam	**Real**	Haqeeqee
Grandfather	Jed	**Easy**	Sahl
Grandmother	Jeda	**Hard**	Sahb
Please	Lou samakht	**Next**	Qadima
Thank you	Shukran	**One**	Wahad
Sorry	Aasif	**Two**	Tineen
New	Jedid	**Three**	Talata
Inside	Daakhil	**Four**	Arbha
Outside	Kharija	**Five**	Hamsa
Different	Okhra	**Six**	Sitta
First	Awwil	**Seven**	Sebba
Last	Akheer	**Eight**	Tmanya
Child	Tafl	**Nine**	Teshah
Man	Rajul	**Ten**	Asrah
Women	Nsaha	**Number**	Rahkam
Week	Sbooah	**Month**	Shaar

To Talk	Yatakelam	**To Drive**	Yasooq
To Walk	Yamshee	**To Pay**	Yadfah
To Run	Yarkad	**To Buy**	Yashtaree
To Sleep	Yanaam	**To Practice**	Yatadrab
To Begin	Yabdaa	**To Prepare**	Istadaa
To Finish	Yantahee	**To Meet**	Yaltaqee
To Drink	Yashrab	**To Fly**	Yatr
To Smoke	Yadakhin	**To Visit**	Yazoor
To Prefer	Yafdal	**To Swim**	Yasbah
To Loose	Mahlul taliq	**To Show**	Yahrad
To Forget	Yanss	**To Know**	Yaraf
To Hold	Yasmad	**To Think**	Yifakar
To Follow	Yitbah	**To Believe**	Amana
To Continue	Yastmarar	**To Love**	Yuhib
To Want	Yurid	**To Like**	Yuhib
To Stay	Iqaama	**To Use**	Yastamil
To Keep	Yafith	**To Try**	Yajarib
To Play	Yalahb	**To Understand**	Yafhaam
To Get	Yasel	**I Have**	Anndi
To Help	Yasaad	**To Happen**	Yahadath
To Go	Yazab	**To Recognize**	Arafa
To Give	Yahat	**To Hear**	Yasmah
To Receive	Yastalm	**To Listen**	Yasmah
To Bring	Jalaba	**To Press**	Yaqwee
To Work	Yahmil	**To Promise**	Yahad
To Hope	Yahamal	**To Choose**	Ikhtar
To Live	Yaskun	**To Arrive**	Yasel
To Find	Yajid	**To Leave**	Yughadeer
To Look	Yantather	**To Leave {Something}**	Yatruk
To Search	Yabhass	**To Do**	Yamel
To See	Yara	**To Order**	Yatlub
To Read	Yikrah	**To Pretend**	Tazahara
To Write	Yaktub	**To Change**	Yughayir
To Learn	Yatalam, Yadrus	**To Be Able To**	Mumkin
To Teach	Yahalam	**To Return**	Yahood, Yarjah
To Take	Yakhud	**To Borrow**	Ista'ara
To Turn on	Wamal	**To Sit**	Yajls
To Turn off	Yatwaqif	**To Need**	Yahtaaj
To Close	Yuqfil	**To Say**	Yaqool
To Put	Yadah	**To Remove**	Yazal
To Allow	Yasmaa	**To Travel**	Yasafar
To Lift	Yaqla	**To Eat**	Yakul
To Open	Yaftah	**To Exchange**	Yughayyir
To Wish	Amal	**To Mix**	Wazub
To Enter	Yadakhl	**To Belong**	Intama
To Come	Dakhala	**To Feel**	Yahees
To Move	Yankal	**To Stop**	Yatawakaf
To Rent	Yasta'jir	**To Ask**	Yasel
To Remember	Yazkar	**To Answer**	Yajeb
To Check	Fahs tibbi	**To Decide**	Yaqrar
To Call	Yatasal	**To Sell**	Yabeeah
To Resemble	Shabaha	**To Wait**	Yantazir

Building Bridges

I Can	Mumkin
I Do	Amal
I Go	Az-ab
I Need	Akhtaj
I Want	Arid
I See	Ara
I Like	Arid
I Say	Aqool
I Talk	Atakalam

Phrases:

I don't speak Arabic
Ana la atakelam Arabya

Ana {I} la {no/don't} atakelam {speak} Arabya {Arabic}

Where can I find the office
Eyyin mumkin yejid al maktab

Eyyin {where} mumkin {can I/ I can} yeijid {to find} al {the} maktab {office}

What do you want to say to me
Maa anta turid yaqool ni

Maa {what} anta {you} turid {[you] want} yaqool {to tell} ni {me}

I want to read the book
Ana urid yakra al kitaab

Ana {I} urid {[I]want} yakra {to read} al {the} kitaab {book}

Pronouns as suffixes with nouns; for example: Book -Kitaab
The book – Al kitaab

Her book – Kitaabuha

His book – Kitaabuhu

Their book – Kitaabuhum

Your book – Kitaabak

Your book {plural} - Kitaabukum

My book – Kaatabi

Our book - Kitaabuma

For Modern Standard Arabic; grammar, pronunciation, accent, conjugation, and sentence structure are recommended but not required for non-Shakespearean speakers. Also the "kh" is essential (refer back to the introduction).

Lebanese Arabic

Lebanese Arabic descends from the traditional Arabic language, though there are many variables that affected the language's development. Although most of the Lebanese speak the language, Arabic remains its written form, despite past attempts by some to make an alphabet. Some people view Lebanese as merely a dialect of Arabic, while others accept the language as unique. Either way, the word connotations vary in both languages, as does its syntax and vocabulary. Lebanese Arabic uses minute Turkish and Aramaic vocabulary, and a little bit of French.

Spoken in: Lebanon and Syria

I	Ana
Me	Ana
My	Tabaae
Mine	La ile
His	Tabauo, la'elo
Him	Howa
Her	Hia
Hers	Tabia
He	Howa
She	Hia
Us	Tabaana
Our	La ilna
With you	Maak
With You {Plural}	Maakoon
With her	Maakeh
With him	Maakouh
With Them	Maaoun
Without me	Balaeh
Without	Balehoum
Without you	Balekeh
Without you {Plural}	Balekoon
Them	Hene
Their	La iloun
You	Inteu
You {Plural}	Inteum
I am	Ana
I was	Ana kenet
I will	Ana lah
Are you	Ente
They	Hene
Without her	Balae he
Without Them	Balae hum
Without Him	Balae
With me	Ma'ey
For you	Laekak
To be	Ya koun
Yours	Laelkoun
We are	Nehna
With us	Maana
Without us	Balena
Who	Meen

What	Shoo	Something	A'aweet
If	Etha	Sometimes	Shagle
Similar	Kama	Somewhere	Bmahal
Where	Ain	Yes	Aeh
Were	Ween	No	Lae
When	Meta	Less	Aaed
Only	Fokat	Instead	Badel
Was	Kent	Including	Maa
Other	Akhar	While	
Since	Manzu	Someone	Hadan
Same	Nafas	Again	Kaman
With	Maa	Away	Baid
Already	Jahez	But	Bas
Together	Sawa	Don't	Mat
Then	Baad theika	Both	Tneinetoun
Than	Aan	Because	Laeno
More	Akhtar	Still, Yet	Baaed
Very	Keteer	Time	Mara
Much, a lot	Keteer	Time	Waeet
From	Min	Time	Saaha
And	Wa	Also, Too	Kameen
Before	Qabl	Around	Hawalee
After	Baad	Never	Abadan
Afterwards	Baaden	Of course	Beltabez
To	La	Here	Huna
The	Al	This	Haida
That	Haida	OK	Taeeb
That	Inou	Just	Bas
Is	B	Although	Law kan
Which	Aya	Through	Makhelal
For	Michen	It is	Heeh
Of	Aan	Everywhere	Ween makeen
Against	Dud	Ready	Jahez
Always	Allatoul	Soon	Areeban
Until	Lawaet	Except	Ila
Everything	Koulna, kulshi	Between	Beenat
Every	Kul	Now	Halaee
Even If	Hata lou	Later	Baadeen
Things	Shashli	Toward	Betejah
There	Hounik	How Much & How Many	Bekam
Into	Bealeb	Neither	Wala wahad
Or	Aw	None	Wala shee
On	Ala	Nobody	Wala hadan
About	Aan	Maybe	Yemkin
How	Kif	Way	Tareele
In	Jouwa	Why	Leesh
Nothing	Walashee	Side	Janab
At	Aan	Everybody	Kull elnas
Almost	Anjae	A Few	Aleel

Small	Sgheir	**Name**	Ism
Big	Kabir	**Last name**	Akher ism
Hot	Sikhun	**What is your name**	Shoo ismaak
Cold	Bared	**How old are you**	Adeesh aoumrak
Up	Fook	**Welcome**	Itadal
Down	Tahat	**Years**	Sneen
Person	Shakes	**Sky**	Sama
People	Nas	**Night**	Beleel
Fast	Sareeaa	**Light**	Daw
Slow	Batee	**Darkness**	Atmeh
Day	Yoom	**Morning**	Sabah
Tomorrow	Bokra	**House**	Beet
Today	El yom	**Car**	Sayara
Yesterday	Embareh	**Left**	Shimal
Good	Mneeh	**Right**	Yameen
Bad	Mamneeh	**Place**	Maahal
Hello	Keefak	**Straight**	Jales
Goodbye	Alla maak	**Parents**	Ahel
How are you	Keefak	**Book**	Kteeb
Nice to meet you	Tasharafna	**Problem**	Mashkleh
Good Night	Tisbah ala kheer	**Behind**	Wara
Good Afternoon	Masa el khir	**Front**	Edam
Good Morning	Sabaho	**Near**	Areeb
Friend	Sahbeh	**Far**	Baeed
Mom	Im	**Sun**	Shames
Dad	Baye	**Better**	Ahsan
Brother	Khayeh	**Worse**	Adrab
Sister	Ikht	**Beautiful**	Helo
Cousin	Ibn amii	**Real**	Anjad
Grandfather	Jido	**Easy**	Hayen
Grandmother	Teta etsito	**Hard**	Asi
Please	Iemool maroof	**Next**	Baadeen
Thank you	Yeslamo	**One**	Wahad
Sorry	Asef	**Two**	Tneen
New	Jdeed	**Three**	Tleteh
Inside	Jowa	**Four**	Arbaa
Outside	Bera	**Five**	Khamseh
Different	Kheer	**Six**	Sita
First	Awal	**Seven**	Sabaa
Last	Akher	**Eight**	Tmeenya
Child	Walad	**Nine**	Tisaa
Man	Rejal	**Ten**	Ashra
Women	Mara	**Number**	Rakem
Week	Jomaa	**Month**	Shaher

To Talk	Tahke	**To Drive**	Souk
To Walk	Tamshe	**To Pay**	Itfah
To Run	Turkoud	**To Buy**	Ishtreh
To Sleep	T'neen	**To Practice**	Laetmaran
To Begin	Baleesh	**To Prepare**	Hadir
To Finish	Khalees	**To Meet**	Itaaraf
To Drink	Tashrab	**To Fly**	Tir
To Smoke	Dakhen	**To Visit**	Azour
To Prefer	Tfadid	**To Swim**	Isbah
To Loose	Dayenh	**To Show**	Farjeh
To Forget	T'insah	**To Know**	Aahref
To Hold	Tamsouk	**To Think**	Fakeer
To Follow	T'elhah	**To Believe**	Azoun
To Continue	T'kafee	**To Love**	Heb
To Want	Bidu	**To Like**	Byejebneh
To Stay	T'ibaa	**To Use**	Istaahmel
To Keep	T'ekoul	**To Try**	Jareeb
To Play	T'illaab	**To Understand**	Laifham
To Get	T'jeeb	**To Have**	Indeeh
To Help	T'saed	**To Happen**	Latseer
To Go	Roohh	**To Recognize**	Laifham
To Give	T'aahte	**To Hear**	Smaaet
To Receive	T'jeeb	**To Listen**	Istamaah
To Bring	Djeeb	**To Press**	Laikbous
To Work	T'ishtughe	**To Promise**	Bou aadak
To Hope	T'amal	**To Choose**	Lanaeeh
To Live	T'iesh	**To Arrive**	Wasalet
To Find	T'laeh	**To Leave**	Faraket
To Look	T'it faras	**To Leave {Something}**	Etrouk
To Search	Fateesh	**To Do**	Aahmoul
To See	Shouf	**To Order**	Lah outloub
To Read	Ikra	**To Pretend**	Lah aamel haleh
To Write	Ektoub	**To Change**	Ghaeyer
To Learn	Intallam	**I Can {no infntv}**	Baa-dir
To Teach	Ahlem	**To Return**	Irjah
To Take	Ekhoud	**To Borrow**	Istaer
To Turn on	Dawee	**To Sit**	La eeoud
To Turn off	Etfee	**To Need**	Lahaouz
To Close	Sakir	**To Say**	La oul
To Put	Hut	**To Remove**	Lah sheel
To Allow	Khalee	**To Travel**	Lasafer
To Lift	Ehmoul	**To Eat**	Laekoul
To Open	Eftah	**To Exchange**	Badeed
To Wish	Yarel	**To Mix**	Laou klout
To Enter	Fout	**To Belong**	Laeehee
To Come	Ejeuh	**To Feel**	Lahees
To Move	Zih	**To Stop**	Lawaeef
To Rent	Estaejeer	**To Ask**	Laesaal
To Remember	Etzakar	**To Answer**	Laeesaal
To Check	Lauofhas	**To Decide**	Lahareer
To Call	Latalfeen	**To Sell**	Labeeh
To Resemble	Lateshbah	**To Wait**	Laountour

Building Bridges

I Can	Ana Baa-dir
I Do	Ana Bamal
I Go	Ana Roohh
I Need	Ana Aiid
I Want	Ana Badi
I See	Ana Shoof
I Like	Ana Hub
I Say	Ana Bhool
I Talk	Ana Bahke

Refer back to Modern Standard Arabic {Classical Arabic} for more information.

Syrian Arabic

Levantine Arabic is a widely known dialect of Modern Standard Arabic, spoken in Syria. Though Levantine Arabic is not the official language of the country, it is spoken very commonly. The dialect is spoken, and does not have a set written form. Levantine Arabic is considered a blend of over 100 Arabic dialects.

Spoken in: Syria, Lebanon, and some parts of Jordan and Israel

I	Ana
Me	Ana
My	Tabaee
Mine	Tabaee
His	Tabaou
Him	Huwe
Her	Heyee
Hers	Tabaeha
He	Huwe
She	Heyyee
Us	Nehne
Our	Tabeana
With you	Maek
With You {Plural}	Maekm
With her	Ma'a
With him	Ma'u
With Them	Mahum
Without me	Mumaei
Without	Muma'a
Without you	Mumaek
Without you {Plural}	Mumaekum
Them	Hum
Their	Tabeahum
You	Enta
You {Plural}	Eentu
I am	Ana
I was	Ana kunt
I will	Ana rah
Are you	Hel enta?
They	Hunne
Without her	Mummaeha
Without Them	Mumaehum
Without Him	Mumaeeu
With me	Maeek
For you	Illak
To be	Takoon
Yours	Tabaek
We are	Nehna
With us	Maeena
Without us	Mumaeena
Who	Meen

What	Shu	**Something**	Sheey
If	Iza	**Sometimes**	Ahyanan
Similar	Mithil	**Somewhere**	Biay makan
Where	Wain	**Yes**	Ey
Were	Kenna	**No**	La
When	Eimta	**Less**	Aeel
Only	Bas	**Instead**	Bidal
Was	Kan	**Including**	Shamel
Other	Tani	**While**	Lamma
Since	Min	**Someone**	Hada
Same	Mithil	**Again**	Marra Tani
With	Maa	**Away**	Rooh baeed
Already	Khales	**But**	Bas
Together	Sawa	**Don't**	Lla taemally
Then	Badein	**Both**	Elitnain
Than	Min	**Because**	Mishan
More	Akthar	**Still**	Baed
Very	Ektheer	**Time**	Mara
Much, a lot	Ektheer	**Time**	Zemaan
From	Min	**Time**	Saa'ha
And	Wa	**Also, Too**	Kaman
Before	Abel	**Around**	Howl
After	Baed	**Never**	Abadan
Afterwards	Baed	**Of course**	Akeed
To	Lil	**Here**	Hown
The	El	**This**	Hath
That	Hathak	**OK**	Ey
That	Ouia	**Just**	Bas
Is	N/A	**Although**	Eza
Which	Ayet	**Through**	Bi---
For	Bi	**It is**	Huwe
Of	Addaish	**Everywhere**	Kel makan
Against		**Ready**	Mustaed
Always	Lilabad	**Soon**	Areeb
Until		**Except**	Mu
Everything	Kil sheey	**Between**	Bain
Every	Kil	**Now**	Hell'a
Even If	Hatta iza	**Later**	Baidain
Things	Sheey (eshya)	**Toward**	Lil
There	Houwneek	**How Much & How Many**	Adish
Into	Ella	**Neither**	Ma shey
Or	Ow	**None**	Ma fee shee
On	Ala	**Nobody**	Ma hada
About	Aen	**Maybe**	Yimken
How	Keef	**Way**	Taree'a
In	Dakhil (bil)	**Why**	Ley
Nothing	Wala shey	**Side**	Janeb
At	Bil	**Everybody**	Kil alnas
Almost	Anjae	**A Few**	Aleel

Small	Izgeer	Name	Ism
Big	Ikbeer	Last name	Ism Akheer
Hot	Showb	What is you name	Shu Ismak
Cold	Berd	How old are you	Addeish omrak
Up	Foo'a	Welcome	Ahlan
Down	Teht	Years	Saneen
Person	Hada	Sky	Yowm
People	Nas	Night	Lail
Fast	Saree'a	Light	Do'a
Slow	Batee'a	Darkness	Muthlim
Day	Yowm	Morning	Subh
Tomorrow	Bukra	House	Bait
Today	Elyowm	Car	
Yesterday	Imbarah	Left	Shimal
Good	Meneeh	Right	Yameen
Bad	Mamineeh	Place	Makan
Hello	Marhaba	Straight	Mustaeem
Goodbye	Ma'a salameh	Parents	Ahel
How are you	Keefek	Book	Kitab
Nice to meet you	Tasharrafna	Problem	Mushkila
Good Night	Tisbah ala khair	Behind	Wara
Good Afternoon	Nahar saeed	Front	Iddam
Good Morning	Sabah elkhair	Near	Areeb
Friend	Sadee'a	Far	Baeed
Mom	Immy	Sun	Shamis
Dad	Baba	Better	Ahsan
Brother	Khayi	Worse	Aswa'
Sister	Ekhti	Beautiful	Hilu
Cousin	Ibn aamy	Real	Haeeieey
Grandfather	Jiddo	Easy	Sahl
Grandmother	Sitto	Hard	Sa'ab
Please	Min fadlik	Next	Tani
Thank you	Yeslamu	One	Wahed
Sorry	Asef	Two	Tanain
New	Jadeed	Three	Talata
Inside	Juwe	Four	Arba'a
Outside	Barrat	Five	Khamsa
Different	Gair	Six	Sitta
First	Awel	Seven	Sab'ah
Last	Akhir	Eight	Tamaniah
Child	Sageer	Nine	Tis'a
Man	Zalimah	Ten	Ashara
Women	Mar'aa	Number	Ra'am
Week	Usbooa	Month	Shaher

To Talk	Ahky	**To Drive**	Asoo'a
To Walk	Amshy	**To Pay**	Adf'a
To Run	Arkad	**To Buy**	Ashtari
To Sleep	Anam	**To Practice**	Atmaran
To Begin	Abd'a	**To Prepare**	Asta'ed
To Finish	Akhalis	**To Meet**	Atarraf
To Drink	Ashrab	**To Fly**	Ateer
To Smoke	Adakhin	**To Visit**	Azoor
To Prefer	Afadel	**To Swim**	Asbah
To Loose	Khasert	**To Show**	Abayen
To Forget	Ansa	**To Know**	A'aref
To Hold	Amsik	**To Think**	Afakar
To Follow	Atab'a	**To Believe**	Asade'a
To Continue	Akammel	**To Love**	Bahib
To Want	Biddy	**To Like**	Bahib
To Stay	Akhali	**To Use**	Astamel
To Keep	Amsik	**To Try**	Bajarreb
To Play	Elab	**To Understand**	Afham
To Get	Akhuth	**To Have**	Aindy
To Help	Asaed	**To Happen**	
To Go	Barooh	**To Recognize**	Befteker
To Give	Ba'athy	**To Hear**	Basma'a
To Receive	Akhuth	**To Listen**	Basm'a
To Bring	Bajeeb	**To Press**	
To Work	A'amel	**To Promise**	Aw'ed
To Hope	Atmanna	**To Choose**	Akhtar
To Live	A'aeesh	**To Arrive**	Waslet
To Find	Ala'eey	**To Leave**	Sibt
To Look	Atul	**To Leave {Something}**	Atruk
To Search	Badawwer	**To Do**	Ba'amal
To See	Batil	**To Order**	Athlub
To Read	A'era	**To Pretend**	Adaeey
To Write	Aktub	**To Change**	Agair
To Learn	Bat'alam	**I Can**	Bi'adar
To Teach	Alim	**To Return**	Araji'a
To Take	Bakhuth	**To Borrow**	Astaeer
To Turn on	Aftah	**To Sit**	B'uad
To Turn off	Bathuffi	**To Need**	Bihtaj
To Close	Ba'effel	**To Say**	Ba'akhuth
To Put	Bahut	**To Remove**	Bazeel
To Allow	Bakhally	**To Travel**	Basafer
To Lift	Barfa'a	**To Eat**	Bakul
To Open	Aftah	**To Exchange**	Abadil
To Wish	Batmanna	**To Mix**	Akhallit
To Enter	Adkhul	**To Belong**	Bakoon
To Come	Bajy	**To Feel**	Bahis
To Move	Uharek	**To Stop**	Uwef
To Rent	Ast'ajer	**To Ask**	As'al
To Remember	Aftaker	**To Answer**	Arud
To Check	Araj'a	**To Decide**	Ahkee
To Call	Atasel	**To Sell**	Abee'a
To Resemble	Bashbah	**To Wait**	Bastanna

Building Bridges

I Can	Bi'adar
I Do	A'amel
I Go	Arooh
I Need	Ahtaj
I Want	Biddy
I See	Batul
I Like	Bahib
I Say	A'ool
I Talk	Bahky

Refer back to Modern Standard Arabic {Classical Arabic} for more information.

Palestinian Arabic

Palestinian Arabic, like many other Middle Eastern languages, is a dialect of the more official Modern Standard Arabic language. However, though various countries have their own dialects, Palestinian Arabic is the most similar to Syrian and Lebanese. With this language, the urban versions are surprisingly not as popular as its rural versions, though urban versions are slowly growing.

Spoken in: The Palestinian controlled territories such as the West Bank and the Gaza Strip, also in Israel, as well as some areas of Lebanon, Syria, Jordan, and parts of Egypt

I	Ana
Me	Ana
My	E-lee
Mine	Tabae
His	Whoa
Him	Whoa
Her	Hiya
Hers	Tabaha
He	Hoo
She	Hiya
Us	Nakhnu
Our	Nakhnu
With you	Maak
With You {Plural}	Ma'akom
With her	Maiya
With him	Mahoo
With Them	Mahoom
Without me	Bi-do-ni
Without	Bi-doon
Without you	Bi-doo-nak
Without you {Plural}	Bi-doon-Kom
Them, They	Hom
Their	El-hom
You	Inta
You {Plural}	Into
I am	Ana
I was	Bakid
I will	Sow-fa
Are you	Ente
We	Ah-na
Without her	Bi-doon-ha
Without Them	Bi-doon-hom
Without Him	Bi-doo-no
With me	Maai
For you	Lilka
To be	Biyus
Yours	Entus
We are	Nah-nu
With us	Ma'a-na
Without us	Bi-doon-na
Who	mein

What	Shoo	Something	E-shee
If	Iza	Sometimes	Ahh-yan-nan
Similar	Sha-beeh	Somewhere	Makan
Where	Wen	Yes	Na'aam
Were	kan	No	La'
When	Metta	Less	a-aal
Only	Bus	Instead	Ba-dal
Was	Baca	Including	Yesh-mal
Other	Guer	While	Bey-na-ma
Since	Men	Someone	Ha-da
Same	Na-fes	Again	Kaman mara
With	Maga	Away	Ba'aeed
Already		But	Wa la kin
Together	Mabaad	Don't	Ma ta'amal
Then		Both	Et-ti-nien
Than	Min	Because	Le a'n-no
More	Asuad	Still, Yet	Liss-sa
Very	Ke-teer	Time	Mara
Much, a lot	Ke-teer	Time	Wa'it
From	Min	Time	Sahah
And	Wa	Also, Too	Kaman, ay-dan
Before	A'-bil	Around	Hawali
After	Ba'ed	Never	Wala mara
Afterwards	Ba'ad-een	Of course	Tab'aan
To	E'-la	Here	Hoon
The	Al	This	Ha-da
That	Ha-dak	OK	Tayeb, mashi
That	Inou	Just	Bes
Is		Although	Ma'aa ino
Which	Ay	Through	Khi-lal
For		It is	Howa
Of	A'an	Everywhere	Kul makan
Against	Did	Ready	Ja-hiz
Always	Dayman	Soon	A'-reeb
Until	Hata	Except	El-la
Everything	Kul-lo	Between	Bein
Every	Kul	Now	Hala
Even If	Hata laow	Later	Ba'adeen
Things	A'shya'a	Toward	Na ho
There	Ho-nak	How Much & How Many	Ad-diesh
Into		Neither	Wala ana
Or	Aow	None	Wala wahid
On	A'la	Nobody	Wala hed
About	A'an	Maybe	Bi-jooz
How	Keef	Way	Taree'
In	Bi	Why	Leish
Nothing	Wala shee	Side	Je-ha
At	Bi	Everybody	Al-jameea'
Almost	Ta'-ree-ban	A Few	Shwee

Small	Sa-gh-er	**Name**	E-sem
Big	Ka-beer	**Last name**	Esmak el akheer
Hot	Shooob	**What is you name**	Eish eismak
Cold	Berd	**How old are you**	Ad-deish om-rak
Up	Fooo'	**Welcome**	Ta fad dal
Down	Ta-hit	**Years**	Sineen
Person	Sha-khis	**Sky**	Sama
People	Nas	**Night**	Leil
Fast	Sareea'	**Light**	Daow
Slow	Ba-tee'	**Darkness**	A'tmeh
Day	Yoom	**Morning**	Soboo7
Tomorrow	Bok-ra	**House**	Beit
Today	El-yoom	**Car**	Sey-ya-ra
Yesterday	Em-ba-reh	**Left**	She-mal
Good	Tayeb	**Right**	Ya-meen
Bad	Sey-ye'	**Place**	Makan
Hello	Marhaba	**Straight**	Dogh-ri
Goodbye	Ma'a esslameh	**Parents**	Ah-hil
How are you	Keefek?	**Book**	Ki-tab
Nice to meet you	It-shar-raf-na	**Problem**	Mosh-ki-la
Good Night	Sa'eedeh	**Behind**	Wara
Good Afternoon		**Front**	Aod-dam
Good Morning	Sabah el khair	**Near**	Jemb
Friend	Sadeeq	**Far**	Ba'aeed
Mom	om-mee	**Sun**	Shams
Dad	A-booy	**Better**	Ah-san
Brother	A-khooy	**Worse**	As-wa'
Sister	Akh-ti	**Beautiful**	Heee-loe
Cousin	Abin a'amee	**Real**	Jed
Grandfather	Sedee	**Easy**	Sa-hil
Grandmother	Sit-tee	**Hard**	Sa-'aeb
Please	Lo samaht	**Next**	Ba'ed
Thank you	Shokran	**One**	Wa-had
Sorry	Aa-sif	**Two**	Ti-nein
New	Ja-deed	**Three**	Ta-la-the
Inside	Joe-wa	**Four**	Ar-ba'aa
Outside	Ber-ra	**Five**	Kham-she
Different	Gh-air	**Six**	Sit-teh
First	Aawal	**Seven**	Seb'aa
Last	Aakhir	**Eight**	Ta-men-yeh
Child	Walad	**Nine**	Tes-'aa
Man	Zalameh	**Ten**	'a-sha-ra
Women	Mara	**Number**	Ra-qam
Week	Os-boo	**Month**	Sha-hir

To Talk	Nihhki	**To Drive**	Soke
To Walk	Mashayae	**To Pay**	Etfah
To Run	yerkod	**To Buy**	Eshtre
To Sleep	Noom	**To Practice**	Ye-ta-der-reb
To Begin	Nabdah	**To Prepare**	Sawae
To Finish	Enkhalis	**To Meet**	Ye-'abel
To Drink	Nishrab	**To Fly**	Tayer
To Smoke	Ndakhin	**To Visit**	Finas
To Prefer	Yee-fed-dil	**To Swim**	Isbakh
To Loose	Nekhsar	**To Show**	Shoof
To Forget	Nsid	**To Know**	Enshoof
To Hold	Yem-sek	**To Think**	Faker
To Follow	Nshoof	**To Believe**	Ensadek
To Continue	Yee-kem-mel	**To Love**	Hob
To Want	Bidi	**To Like**	Bidi
To Stay	Ndal	**To Use**	Yes-ta'a-mel
To Keep	Ndal	**To Try**	Sawi
To Play	Nelab	**To Understand**	Afaam
To Get	Nsawi	**To Have**	Khode
To Help	Nsaada	**To Happen**	Essir
To Go	Rohh	**To Recognize**	Ye-ta-'aaraf
To Give	Atti	**To Hear**	Nisma
To Receive	Bedoum atom	**To Listen**	Nisam
To Bring	Natte	**To Press**	Hotae
To Work	Namel	**To Promise**	Halfae
To Hope	Namel	**To Choose**	Hodae
To Live	Naish	**To Arrive**	Aja
To Find	Nejed	**To Leave**	Hish
To Look	Nshoof	**To Leave {Something}**	Yet-rik e-shee
To Search	Dawar	**To Do**	Sawae
To See	Nshoof	**To Order**	Sawae
To Read	Nkra	**To Pretend**	Tiadar
To Write	Nkhtob	**To Change**	Gayer
To Learn	Ntahallam	**I Can**	Aes-ta-tee'aa
To Teach	Ntahallam	**To Return**	Eizyau
To Take	Nahhood	**To Borrow**	Yes-ta-'aaeer
To Turn on	Tiftah	**To Sit**	Ya' 'oood
To Turn off	Saker	**To Need**	Eikhtag
To Close	Saker	**To Say**	Yahool
To Put	Hot	**To Remove**	Ye-zeeeh
To Allow	Yes-mah	**To Travel**	Safar
To Lift	Yeh-mel	**To Eat**	Ekhul
To Open	Yef-tah	**To Exchange**	Gayer
To Wish	Bidi	**To Mix**	Yakh-lot
To Enter	Rohe	**To Belong**	
To Come	Rohe	**To Feel**	Ye-heesss
To Move	Yo-harrik	**To Stop**	Ye Wa' 'eef
To Rent	Yes-ta'-jer	**To Ask**	Esal
To Remember	Ye-ta-zek-ker	**To Answer**	Ye-jaweb
To Check	Fatnae	**To Decide**	Ye-qar-rir
To Call	Shoofe	**To Sell**	Ya bee'aa
To Resemble	Nadae	**To Wait**	Yes tin na

Building Bridges

I Can	As-ta-teea'aa
I Do	Amaal
I Go	A-rooh
I Need	Ah-taj
I Want	Bidi
I See	Bashoof
I Like	Bahib
I Say	Ba'oool
I Talk	Beh ki

Refer back to Modern Standard Arabic {Classical Arabic} for more information.

Egyptian Arabic

Although the official language of Egypt is Modern Standard Arabic, its people speak Egyptian Arabic. Written in the Arabic alphabet, the language is spoken by over 77 million people throughout the world, though mostly concentrated in Egypt. Unlike Modern Standard Arabic, most people speak Egyptian Arabic at social occasions, though it is also used in some common examples like newspapers and street signs. Egyptian Arabic originated in the areas around Alexandria and Cairo, which have always led the country economically. Historically, the ancient Muslim expeditions to Egypt resulted in an increase in the Arabic language, but shifted back to Egyptian when Muslim troops, speaking an Egyptian dialect, inhabited the area.

Spoken in: Primarily in Egypt as well as other Arabic speaking countries

I	Ana
Me	Melky
My	Tehai
Mine	Tehai
His	Woa
Him	Woa
Her	Hiyaa
Hers	
He	Woaa
She	Hiyaa
Us	Nakhnu
Our	Tabana
With you	Maak
With You {Plural}	Maakoom
With her	Maah
With him	Maae
With Them	Mahoom
Without me	Mingeri
Without	Mingero
Without you	Mingerak
Without you {Plural}	Mingerakoom
Them, They	Hom
Their	Betakhum
You	Anta
You {Plural}	Antum
I am	Ana
I was	Ana Kont
I will	Hamel
Are you	Hal Inta
We	Nakhnu
Without her	Mingera
Without Them	Mingerom
Without Him	Mingero
With me	Maai
For you	Likenta
To be	Lilkom
Yours	Melka
We are	Ekhna
With us	Maana
Without us	Mingerna
Who	Min

What	Maa	**Something**	Ashei
If	Laou	**Sometimes**	Badlowwat
Similar {like}	Misl	**Somewhere**	Meken me
Where	Fein	**Yes**	Laa
Were	Malgood	**No**	Naam
When	Meta	**Less**	Aqal
Only	Fokat	**Instead**	Bedir
Was	Kont	**Including**	Yashmal
Other	Okhra	**While**	Fatra
Since	Min	**Someone**	Khad ma
Same as	Misl Zaee	**Again**	Maratania
With	Maa	**Away**	Baeed
Already		**But**	Lekat
Together	Maa	**Don't**	La
Then	Taala Mayae	**Both**	Intiin
Than	Akhsan	**Because**	Lekan
More	Akhtap	**Still**	Mezel
Very	Keteer	**Time**	Mara
Much, a lot	Keteer	**Time**	Ayem Zemen
From	Min	**Time**	Saaha
And	Wa	**Also, Too**	Kaamin
Before	Baeabel	**Around**	Awaleen
After	Baat	**Never**	Abedan
Afterwards	Baad	**Of course**	Akeed
To	Li	**Here**	Hoona
The	Al	**This**	Daa
That	Dah	**OK**	Hasnan
That	Ouls	**Just**	Dwotee, Alkheen
Is	Hazza	**Although**	
Which	Anhi	**Through**	Minkhilel
For	Le	**It is**	Hazza
Of	Min	**Everywhere**	Kul Imekan
Against	Dedd	**Ready**	Jaaiz
Always	Tamally	**Soon**	Kariban
Until	Lahad	**Except**	Yakbal
Everything	Kul	**Between**	Bin
Every	Kul	**Now**	Tohu, Alkheen, Dilwatee
Even If	Hata Lou	**Later**	Baad
Thing	Ashiae	**Toward**	Tiae
There	Honnak	**How Much & How Many**	Bekam
Into		**Neither**	Leda Waleda
Or	Awo	**None**	Wala Akhad
On	Ala	**Nobody**	Fisnad
About	Ala	**Maybe**	Imkin
How	Keef	**Way**	Tarae
In	Fee	**Why**	Lee
Nothing	Walhaja	**Side**	Nahya
At	Fee	**Everybody**	Kul AlNas
Almost	Anjae	**A Few**	Aleel

English	Translation	English	Translation
Small	Sugair	Name	Ism
Big	Kabeer	Last name	Akharis
Hot	Sukhan	What is your name	Ismakahae
Cold	Bareed	How old are you	Inta kadae
Up	Fo	Welcome	Aalan
Down	Takht	Years	Saanin
Person	Wahad	Sky	Saama
People	Naas	Night	Laila
Fast	Saraa	Light	Noor
Slow	Betilga	Darkness	Zalam
Day	Yom	Morning	Sabaah
Tomorrow	Bokra	House	Bit
Today	Al Yom	Car	Arabya
Yesterday	Ams	Left	Shmaal
Good	Kois	Right	Yamin
Bad	Waish	Place	Mekan
Hello	Marhaba	Straight	Dogri
Goodbye	Ma al salamah	Parents	Ahel
How are you	Kif Halak	Book	Katab
Nice to meet you	Tasharafna	Problem	Mashekel
Good Night	Tisbah al khir	Behind	Wara
Good Afternoon	Masa al khir	In-Front	Bidaam
Good Morning	Sabah al noor	Near	Kareeb
Friend	Sahab	Far	Baeeda
Mom	Hoom	Sun	Shams
Dad	Haboya	Better	Akhsan
Brother	Akh	Worse	Haohash
Sister	Okht	Beautiful	Jamil
Cousin	Ibna am	Real	Khakik
Grandfather	Gidy	Easy	Sahl
Grandmother	Gida	Hard	Saab
Please	Lou samakht	Next	Kadema
Thank you	Shokran	One	Wahad
Sorry	Aasif	Two	Tnien
New	Jedid	Three	Talatae
Inside	Jowa	Four	Harbah
Outside	Bara	Five	Hamsa
Different	Okhra	Six	Sita
First	Awal	Seven	Seba
Last	Akher	Eight	Tmania
Child	Walad	Nine	Tishah
Man	Rajid	Ten	Hasra
Women	Sitt	Number	Nimr
Week	Saboha	Month	Shaar

To Talk	Yikhki	**To Drive**	Yisuu
To Walk	Imshi	**To Pay**	Yitfah
To Run	Yigri	**To Buy**	Yishtaree
To Sleep	Yinahem	**To Practice**	Yitamree
To Begin	Yabda	**To Prepare**	Yahadahar
To Finish	Yakhalas	**To Meet**	Yabel
To Drink	Yashreb	**To Fly**	Yiteer
To Smoke	Yidakhad	**To Visit**	Yazoor
To Prefer	Yemais	**To Swim**	Yasbah
To Loose	Yikhsaar	**To Show**	Yifarog
To Forget	Yinsaa	**To Know**	Yalaam
To Hold	Yimseek	**To Think**	Yafakar
To Follow	Ytba	**To Believe**	Yisadaak
To Continue	Yikama	**To Love**	Yaheb
To Want	Bidu	**To Like**	Yaheb
To Stay	Yohadd	**To Use**	Yistamel
To Keep	Yekhali	**To Try**	Yigarab
To Play	Yetlab	**To Understand**	Yafham
To Get	Yibhaa	**To Have**	Andak
To Help	Mossadda	**To Happen**	Yakhlas
To Go	Roohh	**To Recognize**	Yardak
To Give	Yatee	**To Hear**	Yesmaa
To Receive	Yekhud	**To Listen**	Yesmaa
To Bring	Yigib	**To Press**	Yitbah
To Work	Yishtagal	**To Promise**	Aw'ed
To Hope	Itamana	**To Choose**	Yakhtar
To Live	Aish	**To Arrive**	Yosel
To Find	Yeged	**To Leave**	Yimsee
To Look	Yanzur	**To Leave {Something}**	Teseeb
To Search	Yibkhas	**To Do**	Yamal
To See	Shoof	**To Order**	Yamal
To Read	Yakra	**To Pretend**	Yawari
To Write	Yiktub	**To Change**	Tuvair
To Learn	Tahalem	**I Can** {no infntv}	Akdar
To Teach	Yahalem	**To Return**	Tijah
To Take	Yehud	**To Borrow**	Yistalif
To Turn on	Ywalla li	**To Sit**	Yaad
To Turn off	Yifi	**To Need**	Yikhtag
To Close	Tikfil	**To Say**	Yahool
To Put	Tahud	**To Remove**	Yekhud
To Allow	Tekha	**To Travel**	Yesefur
To Lift	Tushee	**To Eat**	Takhul
To Open	Yaftah	**To Exchange**	Yebedel
To Wish	Yatamana	**To Mix**	Yikhlud
To Enter	Titkhul	**To Belong**	Milq
To Come	Tigi	**To Feel**	Yekhass
To Move	Ymshee	**To Stop**	Yohaff
To Rent	Yagar	**To Ask**	Yesal
To Remember	Yiftikar	**To Answer**	Yegweb
To Check	Yesaal	**To Decide**	Yahkee
To Call	Yikalam	**To Sell**	Yabiyaa
To Resemble	Shaba	**To Wait**	Yantather

Building Bridges

I Can	Akdar
I Do	Amal
I Go	Roohh
I Need	Akhtaj
I Want	Bidi
I See	Shoof
I Like	Uheb
I Say	Aqool
I Talk	Bahhke

Refer back to Modern Standard Arabic (Classical Arabic) for more information.

Moroccan Arabic

Moroccan Arabic is a dialect of Modern Standard Arabic, spoken in countries Algeria, Libya, Tunisia and, of course, Morocco. Since Moroccan Arabic is a dialect, it is more of a spoken language, as Modern Standard Arabic is used for writing and official documents. One aspect of the language that makes it differ from MSA is the use of an "N -", which is used for the verb tense of a first person. Moroccan Arabic is a frequently changing language, as there is no set grammar or vocabulary. This makes the language able to incorporate other languages into its own, without breaking any rules.

Spoken in: Morocco, Algeria, Tunisia, and Libya

I	Ana
Me	Ana
My	Ntaai
Mine	Dialie
His	Dialo
Him	Dialo
Her	Dialha
Hers	Dialhom
He	Howa
She	Hiya
Us	Diiana
Our	Diiana
With you	Maak
With You {Plural}	Maakom
With her	Maahaa
With him	Maaha
With Them	Mahoom
Without me	Bla bya
Without	Bla
Without you	Bla bik
Without you {Plural}	Blakoum
Them, They	Howma
Their	Dialhoum
You	Nta
You {Plural}	Ntumm
I am	Ana
I was	Kont
I will	Khaaoi
Are you	Wash
We	Guna
Without her	Bla biha
Without Them	Bla bihoum
Without Him	Blabih
With me	Maaya
For you	Lyk
To be	Ykoun
Yours	Dyalk
We are	Fin
With us	Mana
Without us	Blabyna
Who	Shkoun

What	Shno	**Something**	Shihaja
If	Ila	**Sometimes**	Baddemarat
Similar	Bhal	**Somewhere**	Shiblassa
Where	Fine	**Yes**	Ihh
Were		**No**	Laa
When	Foukash	**Less**	Kll
Only	Khii	**Instead**	Blast
Was	Kan	**Including**	Dakhla
Other	Wahdakhrin	**While**	Foukash
Since	Mnin	**Someone**	Shiwahd
Same	Bhale	**Again**	Awtani
With	Maae	**Away**	Baaid
Already		**But**	Walakin
Together	Bjouj {2 ppl} Bina {3+ ppl}	**Don't**	Matt
Then	Ou	**Both**	Bjouj
Than	Mn	**Because**	Lahkash
More	Zid	**Still**	Mazall
Very	Bzaf	**Time**	Mrat
Much, a lot	Bzaf	**Time**	Wokt
From	Mn	**Time**	Saae
And	Ou	**Also, Too**	Ii
Before	Qabel	**Around**	Doura
After	Baad	**Never**	Maamrie
Afterwards	Mnbaad	**Of course**	Oushno
To	Li	**Here**	Hna
The	Li	**This**	Hada
That	Hada	**OK**	Ihh, waja
That	Dakhshi	**Just**	Yalahh
Is		**Although**	Htta
Which	Fin	**Through**	Foust
For		**It is**	Wash
Of		**Everywhere**	Koula blassa
Against	Dadh	**Ready**	Wajd
Always	Dima	**Soon**	Krrib
Until	Hta	**Except**	Ila
Everything	Koulshi	**Between**	Binat
Every		**Now**	Dabba
Even If	Htaila	**Later**	Mnbaad
Things	Hajajs	**Toward**	Hta
There	Lihih	**How Much & How Many**	Shaal
Into	Fee	**Neither**	Tawahd
Or	Oula	**None**	Walo
On	Fee	**Nobody**	Tawahij
About	Ala	**Maybe**	Ymkn
How	Kif	**Way**	Tarika
In	Fee	**Why**	Alach
Nothing	Walo	**Side**	Giha
At	Maae	**Everybody**	Koulwahad
Almost	Krib	**A Few**	Shwiya
Small	Skhir	**Name**	Smiaa
Big	Kbir	**Last name**	Kniya

Hot	Skoun	What is you name	Smitak
Cold	Bard	How old are you	Shall fee omrik
Up	Fouk	Welcome	Marhaba
Down	That	Years	Awam
Person	Ibnadm	Sky	Smaae
People	Bnadm	Night	Lile
Fast	Bzarba	Light	Doue
Slow	Bchouya	Darkness	Douloumat
Day	Nhar	Morning	Sabah
Tomorrow	Gada	House	Dar
Today	Luoum	Car	Tounoubil
Yesterday	Lbarah	Left	Lisr
Good	Mzyan	Right	Limn
Bad	Khayb	Place	Blaca
Hello	Ahallan	Straight	Nichan
Goodbye	Bslama	Parents	Walidin
How are you	Fink	Book	Kitab
Nice to meet you	Mtchrfin	Problem	Mouchkhil
Good Night	Tisb al khir	Behind	Mour
Good Afternoon	Msalkhir	Front	Koudam
Good Morning	Sabah al khir	Near	Krib
Friend	Shab	Far	Baiid
Mom	Mama	Sun	Chmch
Dad	Baba	Better	Hassane
Brother	Khouya	Worse	Kfss
Sister	Khty	Beautiful	Zouine
Cousin	Ouldamti	Real	Bsahh
Grandfather	Bassidi	Easy	Sahl
Grandmother	Milala	Hard	Safib
Please	Afak	Next	Lakhour
Thank you	Shoukran	One	Ouad
Sorry	Smahli	Two	Jouje
New	Jdid	Three	Tilata
Inside	Dkhil	Four	Kbaae
Outside	Alabra	Five	Khamsa
Different	Mbdl	Six	Sta
First	Loul	Seven	Sbaa
Last	Lkhr	Eight	Tmnia
Child	Drie	Nine	Tsoud
Man	Rajl	Ten	Achra
Women	Mraae	Number	Nmari
Week	Simana	Month	Shoura

To Talk	Tanhdar	**To Drive**	Tansouk
To Walk	Tanmchi	**To Pay**	Tannakhalass
To Run	Tangri	**To Buy**	Tanbiee
To Sleep	Tanasse	**To Practice**	Tantdrb
To Begin	Tanbda	**To Prepare**	Tanoujad
To Finish	Tankmal	**To Meet**	Tantlaka
To Drink	Tanchrb	**To Fly**	Tantir
To Smoke	Tanmkie	**To Visit**	Tanzour
To Prefer	Tanbrhi	**To Swim**	Tanoum
To Loose	Tannakhsr	**To Show**	Tanouri
To Forget	Tansa	**To Know**	Tanaraf
To Hold	Tankbat	**To Think**	Tanfkr
To Follow	Tantbare	**To Believe**	Tantik
To Continue	Tankmal	**To Love**	Tanbrie
To Want	Tanbgie	**To Like**	Tanbire
To Stay	Tanglass	**To Use**	Tanndir
To Keep	Tannakhbt	**To Try**	Tanjrab
To Play	Tanlaab	**To Understand**	Tannfham
To Get	Tanchd	**To Have**	Dialie
To Help	Tanaoun	**To Happen**	Tanwakaae
To Go	Tannmchi	**To Recognize**	Tantraff
To Give	Tanatti	**To Hear**	Tansmae
To Receive	Tankbt	**To Listen**	Tantsnt
To Bring	Tanoib	**To Press**	Tanbrk
To Work	Tannakdm	**To Promise**	Tantshlaf
To Hope	Tannilab	**To Choose**	Tanazal
To Live	Tannich	**To Arrive**	Tannousal
To Find	Tanklb	**To Leave**	Tanmchi
To Look	Tanchouf	**To Leave {Something}**	Tanmchi
To Search	Tanklb	**To Do**	Tandire
To See	Tankhouf	**To Order**	Tannilab
To Read	Tannkhra	**To Pretend**	Tandirrassi
To Write	Tannktb	**To Change**	Tanbdke
To Learn	Tanntlam	**I Can**	Ana Tankad
To Teach	Tankiri	**To Return**	Tannarjae
To Take	Tanhdar	**To Borrow**	Tantsalf
To Turn on	Tannoud	**To Sit**	Tannklass
To Turn off	Tandfie	**To Need**	Tannbkhi
To Close	Tansaad	**To Say**	Tanngoul
To Put	Tanhatt	**To Remove**	Tannbdal
To Allow	Tankhalli	**To Travel**	Tansafar
To Lift	Tanhazz	**To Eat**	Tannakoul
To Open	Tanhall	**To Exchange**	Tan bdle
To Wish	Tanntlb	**To Mix**	Tannkalt
To Enter	Tannikhoul	**To Belong**	Tannbtani
To Come	Tangie	**To Feel**	Tanhass
To Move	Tannrhal	**To Stop**	Tanoukaf
To Rent	Tankrie	**To Ask**	Tansoule
To Remember	Tannakle	**To Answer**	Tanwajeb
To Check	Tansoul	**To Decide**	Tanfkr
To Call	Tannahdar	**To Sell**	Tanbiie
To Resemble	Tannbdal	**To Wait**	Tantsana

Building Bridges

I Can	Ana Tankad
I Do	Ana Tandire
I Go	Ana Tannmchi
I Need	Ana Tannbkhi
I Want	Ana Tanbgie
I See	Ana Tankhouf
I Like	Ana Tanbire
I Say	Ana Tanngoul
I Talk	Ana Tanhdar

Refer back to Modern Standard Arabic {Classical Arabic} for more information.
Conjugation may be slightly different in Moroccan Arabic.

Iraqi Arabic

Iraqi Arabic is the dialect of Arabic that is used in Iraq. Iraqi Arabic is quite similar in spelling and pronunciation to its neighboring country's form of Arabic called Kuwaiti Arabic. This is one of the most difficult and complex varieties of Arabic, at a similar level to other hard Arabic dialects such as Hijazi and Yemeni. This variety of Arabic used today may have the strongest roots to the Arabic spoken by the Prophet Muhammad according to some, because it is claimed that it resembles Muhammad's Arabic closest in pronunciation among the varieties of Arabic around today.

Spoken in: Iraq, Saudi Arabia, and other Gulf States

I	Ana
Me	Ana
My	Maly
Mine	Maly
His	Malu
Him	Hoowee
Her	Heyee
Hers	Mala
He	Hoowee
She	Heyee
Us	Nehna
Our	Malna
With you	Wayak
With You {Plural}	Wayakem
With her	Wayaha
With him	Wayanu
With Them	Wayahem
Without me	Belaana
Without	Bela
Without you	Belainta
Without you {Plural}	Belaintim
Them, They	Himie
Their	Malem
You	Inta
You {Plural}	Intim
I am	Ana
I was	Kintu
I will	Hal Inta
Are you	Inta
We	Nehna
Without her	Belahiyi
Without Them	Belahimi
Without Him	Belahuwi
With me	Weyayi
For you	Khatalik
To be	Akun
Yours	Malak
We are	Nehna
With us	Weyana
Without us	Belanehna
Who	Meny

What	Eshkun	**Something**	Fekheni
If	Ida	**Sometimes**	Nubat
Similar	Tishba	**Somewhere**	Fedimkan
Where	Ween	**Yes**	Ee
Were	Kina	**No**	La
When	Emta	**Less**	Akal
Only	Bes	**Instead**	Bimkan
Was	Kanet	**Including**	Weeya
Other	Reer	**While**	Zman
Since	Min	**Someone**	Wehed
Same	Methil	**Again**	Nobalakh
With	Wiya	**Away**	Rahet
Already		**But**	Ila
Together	Sewa	**Don't**	Letsowee
Then	Baden	**Both**	Kila
Than	Min	**Because**	Kef
More	Esyed	**Still, Yet**	Bes
Very	Kilish	**Time**	Kemara
Much, a lot	Katir	**Time**	Hawa
From	Min	**Time**	Kemsaah
And	Weya	**Also, Too**	Hemi
Before	Kabel	**Around**	Bessayeh
After	Ekib	**Never**	Welah
Afterwards	Baden	**Of course**	Helbet
To	El	**Here**	Honee
The	Al	**This**	Hayee
That	Hediki	**OK**	Okey
That	Hadack	**Just**	Ma
Is	El	**Although**	Kazalek
Which	Heyee	**Through**	Deyn
For	Minataraf	**It is**	Hayee
Of	Min	**Everywhere**	Kilimkan
Against	Zhid	**Ready**	Hather
Always	Kilwact	**Soon**	Bilajel
Until	Leemtah	**Except**	Yegbl
Everything	Koola	**Between**	Bein
Every	Kela	**Now**	Hassa
Even If	Hati eza	**Later**	Baden
Things	Shenat	**Toward**	Ila
There	Whonik	**How Much & How Many**	Eshkad
Into	Biya	**Neither**	Welah
Or	O	**None**	Makoo
On	Ala	**Nobody**	Mahad
About	Kazalek	**Maybe**	Belki
How	Eshlon	**Way**	Tarik
In	Bhiya	**Why**	Leish
Nothing	Makoo	**Side**	Safha
At	Ala	**Everybody**	Kilim
Almost	Takriban	**A Few**	Shweyah

Small	Zkheyer	Name	Isim
Big	Kabir	Last name	Ism Ekheer
Hot	Har	What is your name	Esh-isimak
Cold	Bared	How old are you	Eshkadimrak
Up	Fock	Welcome	Ahlan
Down	Jawa	Years	Sneene
Person	Admi	Sky	Shamiyim
People	Awadem	Night	Lel
Fast	Bilajel	Light	Thawah
Slow	Yawash	Darkness	Lel
Day	Nehar	Morning	Sabah
Tomorrow	Rada	House	Beit
Today	Yom	Car	Seyara
Yesterday	Bohi	Left	Yisrah
Good	Malih	Right	Yimnah
Bad	Mamlih	Place	Mikan
Hello	Hallow	Straight	Adel
Goodbye	Maalsalama	Parents	Imiaboya
How are you	Eshlonak	Book	Katab
Nice to meet you	Atsharaf	Problem	Eskal
Good Night	Tisbah elkhir	Behind	Khalf
Good Afternoon	Sbahelnoor	Front	Kedam
Good Morning	Sbahelkher	Near	Sob
Friend	Sadik	Far	Baid
Mom	Im	Sun	Shams
Dad	Eb	Better	Ahsen
Brother	Ekh	Worse	Aswa'
Sister	Ekht	Beautiful	Helwah
Cousin	Ebinam	Real	Sidik
Grandfather	Siyad	Easy	Sehel
Grandmother	Sity	Hard	Sa-id
Please	Tefathal	Next	Baden
Thank you	Shookran	One	Wahed
Sorry	Leahfoo	Two	Thenen
New	Jadid	Three	Talatah
Inside	Dakhil	Four	Arabah
Outside	Barah	Five	Hamsah
Different	Rershikil	Six	Sitah
First	Awal	Seven	Sebah
Last	Akhar	Eight	Thamini
Child	Walad	Nine	Tisah
Man	Rajal	Ten	Ashrah
Women	Marah	Number	Nimar
Week	Sabooh	Month	Sheher

To Talk	Yahki	**To Drive**	Yesuk
To Walk	Yamshi	**To Pay**	Yitfah
To Run	Yarkath	**To Buy**	Yishtari
To Sleep	Yenam	**To Practice**	Yatmarran
To Begin	Yestebdi	**To Prepare**	Yehadir
To Finish	Yekhales	**To Meet**	Yelaky
To Drink	Yeshrab	**To Fly**	Yetir
To Smoke	Yedakhin	**To Visit**	Yazoor
To Prefer	Yafadel	**To Swim**	Yesbah
To Loose	Yekhsar	**To Show**	Yerwi
To Forget	Yensah	**To Know**	Yeref
To Hold	Yilzem	**To Think**	Yeftekir
To Follow	Yatab'a	**To Believe**	Yesadek
To Continue	Yakhalis	**To Love**	Yeheb
To Want	Yirid	**To Like**	Yeajib
To Stay	Yethel	**To Use**	Yestaemil
To Keep	Yekhaly	**To Try**	Yijashed
To Play	Yilab	**To Understand**	Yiftehem
To Get	Yakhed	**To Have**	Yekunindi
To Help	Yiawen	**To Happen**	Yesir
To Go	Yewooh	**To Recognize**	
To Give	Yetee	**To Hear**	Yismah
To Receive	Yakhed	**To Listen**	Yismah
To Bring	Yejib	**To Press**	Yedus
To Work	Yishtahrel	**To Promise**	Kawel
To Hope	Yatmanna	**To Choose**	Yintekheb
To Live	Yehyee	**To Arrive**	Yusal
To Find	Yeshuf	**To Leave**	Yeruh
To Look	Yeayin	**To Leave {Something}**	Yekhali
To Search	Yedawir	**To Do**	Yesowi
To See	Yeayen	**To Order**	Yeamir
To Read	Yikah	**To Pretend**	
To Write	Yikhteb	**To Change**	Yebedel
To Learn	Yedres	**I Can {no infntv}**	Akdar
To Teach	Yaalem	**To Return**	Yerajah
To Take	Yakhed	**To Borrow**	Yakhed
To Turn on	Yeftah	**To Sit**	Yakid
To Turn off	Yesed	**To Need**	Yerid
To Close	Yesed	**To Say**	Yekul
To Put	Yehaty	**To Remove**	Yeshil
To Allow	Yekhaly	**To Travel**	Yesafir
To Lift	Yejir	**To Eat**	Yakil
To Open	Yiftah	**To Exchange**	Yeebedel
To Wish	Yatmanna	**To Mix**	Yikhlit
To Enter	Yitkhil	**To Belong**	Mil
To Come	Yejee	**To Feel**	Yehes
To Move	Yemed	**To Stop**	Yeewakuf
To Rent	Yasta jir	**To Ask**	Yeesayal
To Remember	Yeftekir	**To Answer**	Yeejaweb
To Check	Yebdik	**To Decide**	Yeeftakir
To Call	Yekhabir	**To Sell**	Yeebih
To Resemble	Yeshbeh	**To Wait**	Yestandir

Building Bridges

I Can	Akdar
I Do	Asowee
I Go	Awooh
I Need	Mihtaj
I Want	Arid
I See	Aiyin
I Like	Aheb
I Say	Akool
I Talk	Ahki

Refer back to Modern Standard Arabic {Classical Arabic} for more information.

Saudi (Hijazi) Arabic

Like every other Middle Eastern nation, the official language of Saudi Arabia is Modern Standard Arabic. Each country has its own dialects, though MSA unifies them all and makes them able to communicate which each other almost flawlessly. Saudi Arabia houses three dialects, the main one being Najdi. Najdi is spoken is the middle of Saudi Arabia, and is considered an upper class dialect and the royal family speaks the language. Another dialect in Saudi Arabia is Gulf Arabic, also called Shargi. Shargi is found is mostly the Eastern areas of the country. The third dialect is Hijazi Arabic, which is spoken in the Western area of Saudi Arabia. Hijazi Arabic is the most common and popular dialect in the Saudi Peninsula, and it is also used as the main means of communication. For example, much of the Saudi Arabian lifestyle is conveyed with the language with regards to trade and government.

Spoken in: Saudi Arabia and other Gulf States

I	Ana
Me	Ana
My	Haggi
Mine	Haggi
His	Haggu
Him	Huwa
Her	Heya
Hers	Haggaha
He	Huwa
She	Heyya
Us, We	Ahna
Our	Haggana
With you	Maek
With You {Plural}	Maakum
With her	Maeha
With him	Ma'ah
With Them	Mahum
Without me	Mindooni
Without	Mindoon
Without you	Mindoonak
Without you {Plural}	Mindoonikum
Them, They	Hum, Humma
Their	Haagahum
You	Ent
You {Plural}	Eentum
I am	Ana
I was	Ana kunt
I will	Ana rah
Are you	Hel Ent?
Without her	Mindoonaha
Without Them	Mindoonihum
Without Him	Mindoonu
With me	Maeek
For you	Lak
To be	Takoon
Yours	Haggak
We are	Ehna
With us	Maeena
Without us	Mindoonina
Who	Men

What	Aish	Something	Shai
If	Etha	Sometimes	Ahyanan
Similar	Zay	Somewhere	Biay mahel
Where	Fain	Yes	Eiwa
Were	Kun	No	La'a
When	Mita	Less	Agal
Only	Bas	Instead	Badel
Was	Kan	Including	Mitadamen
Other	thani	While	Lamma
Since	Min	Someone	Ahad
Same	Zay	Again	Marra Thani
With	Ma'a	Away	Rooh Baeed
Already	Khalas	But	Bas
Together	Ma'a baed	Don't	La tisaawy
Then	Baed	Both	elithnain
Than	Min	Because	Ashan
More	Kaman	Still	Lissa
Very	Marra	Time	Mara
Much, a lot	Marra	Time	Zemaan
From	Min	Time	Saa'ha
And	Wa	Also, Too	Kaman
Before	Gabel	Around	Howl
After	Baed	Never	Abadan
Afterwards	Baed	Of course	Taba'an
To	Lil	Here	Henna
The	El	This	Hatha
That	Dole	OK	Tayeb
That	Inou	Just	Bas
Is	N/A	Although	Etha
Which	Ayet	Through	Bi--
For	Bi	It is	Huwa
Of	BiKam	Everywhere	Kul makan
Against	Dud	Ready	Mustaed
Always	Lilabad	Soon	Gareeb
Until		Except	Mu
Everything	Kul shay	Between	Bain
Every	Kul	Now	Dahain
Even If	Hatta itha	Later	Baedain
Things	Shay (ashya'a)	Toward	Lil
There	Henna	How Much & How Many	Kam
Into	Ella	Neither	Wella shay
Or	wellah	None	Ma fee shay
On	Foog	Nobody	Ma ahad
About	Aen	Maybe	Yimkan
How	Kaif	Way	Tareeg
In	Juwwa	Why	Lasih
Nothing	Wala shay	Side	Janeb
At	Bil	Everybody	Kul alnas
Almost	Anjae	A Few	Aleel

Small	Sageey	Name	Ism
Big	Kabeer	Last name	Ism Akheer
Hot	Har	What is you name	Aish Ismak
Cold	Bared	How old are you	Kum omrak
Up	Fooq	Welcome	Hala
Down	Tahat	Years	Saneen
Person	Ahad	Sky	Yowm
People	Nas	Night	Lail
Fast	Saree'a	Light	Noor
Slow	Bateeg	Darkness	Muthlim
Day	Yowm	Morning	Sabah
Tomorrow	Bukra	House	Bait
Today	Elyowm	Car	Sayyarah
Yesterday	Amis	Left	Shimal
Good	Kuwais	Right	Yameen
Bad	Mukawais	Place	Makan
Hello	Ya hala	Straight	Mustageem
Goodbye	Ma'a salamah	Parents	Ahel
How are you	Kaifak	Book	Kitab
Nice to meet you	Tasharafna	Problem	Mushkila
Good Night	Tisbah ala khair	Behind	Wara
Good Afternoon	Nahar saeed	Front	Guddam
Good Morning	Sabah elkhair	Near	Gareeb
Friend	Sahib	Far	Baeed
Mom	Mama	Sun	Shams
Dad	Baba	Better	Ahsan
Brother	Akhy	Worse	Aswa'
Sister	Okhity	Beautiful	Jameel
Cousin	Ibn aamy	Real	Hageegy
Grandfather	Jiddy	Easy	Sahil
Grandmother	Jadda	Hard	Sa'ab
Please	Min fadlik	Next	Thani
Thank you	Shukran	One	Wahed
Sorry	Asef	Two	Ithnain
New	Jadeed	Three	Thalatha
Inside	Juwa	Four	Arba'a
Outside	Barra	Five	Khamsa
Different	Gair	Six	Sitta
First	Awel	Seven	Sab'ah
Last	Akhir	Eight	Thananiah
Child	Sageer	Nine	Tis'a
Man	Rijjal	Ten	Ashara
Women	Hurma	Number	Ragam
Week	Usbooa	Month	Shaher

To Talk	Atkalam	**To Drive**	Asoog
To Walk	Amshy	**To Pay**	Adf'a
To Run	Arkaad	**To Buy**	Ashtari
To Sleep	Anam	**To Practice**	Atmarran
To Begin	Abd'a	**To Prepare**	Asta'ed
To Finish	Akhalis	**To Meet**	Atarraf
To Drink	Ashrab	**To Fly**	Ateer
To Smoke	Adakhin	**To Visit**	Azoor
To Prefer	Afadel	**To Swim**	Asbah
To Loose	Khasert	**To Show**	Abayen
To Forget	Ansa	**To Know**	A'aref
To Hold	Amsik	**To Think**	Afaker
To Follow	Atab'a	**To Believe**	Asadeg
To Continue	Akhalis	**To Love**	Uhib
To Want	Abga	**To Like**	Uhib
To Stay	Akhali	**To Use**	Asta'amel
To Keep	Amsik	**To Try**	Ajarreb
To Play	Alab	**To Understand**	Afham
To Get	Bajeeb	**To Have**	Aindy
To Help	Asaed	**To Happen**	
To Go	Barooh	**To Recognize**	A'aref
To Give	A'athy	**To Hear**	Basma'a
To Receive	Akhuth	**To Listen**	Basm'a
To Bring	Bajeeb	**To Press**	
To Work	Ashtagil	**To Promise**	Aw'ed
To Hope	Atmanna	**To Choose**	Akhtar
To Live	A'aeesh	**To Arrive**	Waselt
To Find	Alagy	**To Leave**	Tale'at
To Look	Ashoof	**To Leave {Something}**	Atruk
To Search	Adawwer	**To Do**	Assawy
To See	Shoof	**To Order**	Athlub
To Read	Agra	**To Pretend**	Adaeey
To Write	Aktub	**To Change**	Agair
To Learn	Atalam	**I Can**	Agdar
To Teach	Alim	**To Return**	Arajji'a
To Take	Aakhuth	**To Borrow**	Astaeer
To Turn on	Ashtagil	**To Sit**	Ajles
To Turn off	Bathuffi	**To Need**	Ahtaj
To Close	Basakker	**To Say**	Agool
To Put	Ahut	**To Remove**	Asheel
To Allow	Akhally	**To Travel**	Asafer
To Lift	Asheel	**To Eat**	akul
To Open	Aftah	**To Exchange**	Abadil
To Wish	Batmanna	**To Mix**	Akhallit
To Enter	Adkhul	**To Belong**	Bakoon
To Come	Ajy	**To Feel**	Ahis
To Move	Uharek	**To Stop**	Awgaf
To Rent	Ast'ajer	**To Ask**	As'al
To Remember	Aftaker	**To Answer**	Arud
To Check	Araje'a	**To Decide**	Ahkee
To Call	Atsal	**To Sell**	Abee'a
To Resemble	Biyeshbas	**To Wait**	Astanni

Building Bridges

I Can	Agdar
I Do	Assawy
I Go	Arooh
I Need	Ahtaj
I Want	Abga
I See	Bashoof
I Like	Ahub
I Say	Agool
I Talk	Atakallam

Refer back to Modern Standard Arabic {Classical Arabic} for more information.

Chapter 3:
Indo-Iranian Languages

- Farsi
- Pashto

Farsi

Buying magic carpets isn't what Persia is known for, as Persian is a widely used language throughout the Middle East. The country where Persian, also known as Farsi, is most spoken is in Iran. However it is also spoken in countries such as Iraq, Bahrain, Uzbekistan, Azerbaijan, Armenia, Afghanistan, Southern Russia, Tajikistan, Iran, and neighboring countries. Throughout history many cultures have incorporated Persian into their society. For instance, for some time it was widely used as a second language in the Indian subcontinent. Persian also incorporates many words from closely related languages such as Greek and Arabic that were introduced to the language over time. The language has also developed in other ways such as incorporating new words and idioms into Persian from technological developments like any other language.

Spoken: Iran (Persia), Afghanistan, Tajikistan

I	Man
Me	Man
My	Moyn
Mine	Malaman
His	Hoo
Him	Hoo
Her	Hoo
Hers	Hoo
He	Hoo
She	Hoo
Us	Maa
Our	Maa
With you	Ba shoma
With You {Plural}	Ba shoma
With her	Baao
With him	Bao
With Them	Baanha
Without me	Bidon man
Without	Bidona
Without you	Bidoneshama
Without you {Plural}	Bidoneshama
Them, They	Anha
Their	Anha
You	Shema
You {Plural}	Shema
I am	Maan hastam, Maan daram
I was	Maan boodam
I will	
Are you	Shama hasdid
We	Ma
Without her	Bidone ao
Without Them	Bidone anha
Without Him	Bidon ao
With me	Boman
For you	Barayeh shoma
To be	Bodan
Yours	Malae shema
We are	Ma hastim
With us	Ba ma
Without us	Bidon ma
Who	Key

What	Che	**Something**	Baazi chizha
If	Aghar	**Sometimes**	Baazi vaghtah
Similar	Shabeh	**Somewhere**	Baazi jaha
Where	Koja	**Yes**	Baleh
Were	Bodan	**No**	Na
When	Chemogheh	**Less**	Kaam
Only	Faghat	**Instead**	Brjayeh
Was	Bood	**Including**	Hamrav
Other	Digar	**While**	Tazamanikeh
Since	As vaghati	**Someone**	Shakhsi
Same	Shabeh	**Again**	Dobareh
With	Ba	**Away**	Duor
Already	Hamaknoon	**But**	Amaa
Together	Baham	**Don't**	Na
Then	Chemoghe	**Both**	Hardo
Than	Targeh	**Because**	Baray in keh
More	Ziyad	**Still, Yet**	Hanooz
Very	Ziyad	**Time**	Vaghat
Much, a lot	Ziyad	**Time**	Zaman
From	Az	**Time**	Saaha
And	Va	**Also, Too**	Hamchanin
Before	Ghable	**Around**	Dorvar
After	Baadan	**Never**	Hargez
Afterwards	Baadan	**Of course**	Albeteh
To	Beh	**Here**	Ingah
The		**This**	In
That	Aon	**OK**	Bale
That	Onkee	**Just**	Faghat
Is	Kodam	**Although**	Hata agear
Which	Ba	**Through**	
For	Barayne	**It is**	In hast
Of	Az	**Everywhere**	Harga
Against	Moghabel	**Ready**	Hazer
Always	Hamesheh	**Soon**	Zood
Until	Tavaghtee	**Except**	Bejooz
Everything	Hame chiz	**Between**	Miyan
Every	Har	**Now**	Halah
Even If	Hata ajar	**Later**	Ba dan
Things	Chiz	**Toward**	Betaraphe
There	Anja	**How Much & How Many**	Che andaze, Chanta
Into	Dakhel shodan	**Neither**	Hichkodam
Or	Ya	**None**	Hichkodam
On	Royeh	**Nobody**	Hichshakhsi
About	Darbareh	**Maybe**	Agar
How	A ya	**Way**	Miyam
In	Dakhel	**Why**	Chera
Nothing	Hich chiz	**Side**	Taraf
At		**Everybody**	Herkasi, Har shakhsi
Almost	Taghriban	**A Few**	Chanta

Small	Kojek	Name	Esm
Big	Bozork	Last name	Esm famil
Hot	Biarm	What is your name	Namae shema khae
Cold	Sard	How old are you	Shema chand saletanae
Up	Balla	Welcome	Khosamadid
Down	Paine	Years	Salhaa
Person	Shachs	Sky	Osaman
People	Mardoon	Night	Shab
Fast	Tond	Light	Rashon
Slow	Yavosh	Darkness	Tariq
Day	Ruz	Morning	Sob
Tomorrow	Fardoh	House	Hanae
Today	Emroz	Car	Machin
Yesterday	Diroz	Left	Chap
Good	Khob	Right	Rast
Bad	Yoad	Place	Makann
Hello	Saalam	Straight	Mostaghim
Goodbye	Khudafis	Parents	Famil
How are you	Chetori halle shema	Book	Katab
Nice to meet you	Khoshalem azdidan shema	Problem	Mashkilat
Good Night	Shabkhir	Behind	Aghab
Good Afternoon	Asbkhir	Front	Jelo
Friend	Sobkhir	Near	Nasdik
Good Morning	Dost	Far	Dur
Mom	Mader	Sun	Khorshid
Dad	Pader	Better	Behtar
Brother	Brother	Worse	Betarr
Sister	Khoder	Beautiful	Ziba
Cousin	Amou	Real	Sahi
Grandfather	Pedarbozork	Easy	Sadae
Grandmother	Marabozork	Hard	Sacht
Please	Lot fan	Next	Digar
Thank you	Modshkira	One	Yek
Sorry	Motasifa	Two	Do
New	Jadid	Three	Se
Inside	Dakhel	Four	Khar
Outside	Kharij	Five	Panj
Different	Mokhtarif	Six	Shish
First	Aval	Seven	Haft
Last	Akher	Eight	Hasht
Child	Bache	Nine	Noo
Man	Mard	Ten	Daa
Women	Zaan	Number	Shemaraei
Week	Hafti	Month	Maa

To Talk	Sohbat	**To Drive**	Ranande
To Walk	Raftan	**To Pay**	Pardakhtan
To Run	Davidan	**To Buy**	Kharidan
To Sleep	Khabidon	**To Practice**	Tamerin
To Begin	Shrou	**To Prepare**	Amadeh
To Finish	Tamam	**To Meet**	Molaghat
To Drink	Nushidan	**To Fly**	Parvaz
To Smoke	Dud	**To Visit**	Molaghat
To Prefer	Tarji dadan	**To Swim**	Shenah
To Loose	Azdast dadan	**To Show**	Neshan dadan
To Forget	Faramosh	**To Know**	Denestan
To Hold	Negya doshtan	**To Think**	Fekr kardan
To Follow	Dombal	**To Believe**	Baver
To Continue	Edome dadan	**To Love**	Ashegh
To Want	Khostan	**To Like**	Dost
To Stay	Mandan	**To Use**	Estfade
To Keep	Negah dashtan	**To Try**	Koshesh
To Play	Bozi	**To Understand**	Fahmedan
To Get	Griftan	**To Have**	Dashtan
To Help	Komak	**To Happen**	Etefagh
To Go	Raftan	**To Recognize**	Targeh dadan
To Give	Dudan	**To Hear**	Shonofian
To Receive	Daryaft	**To Listen**	Goosh dadan
To Bring	Awardan	**To Press**	Feshar
To Work	Kar	**To Promise**	Ghole
To Hope	Arzou	**To Choose**	Entekhab
To Live	Zendegi	**To Arrive**	Vard shodan
To Find	Payeda	**To Leave**	Raftan
To Look	Nega	**To Leave {Something}**	Begozar
To Search	Peyda kardan	**To Do**	Kardan
To See	Didan	**To Order**	Cefaresh
To Read	Khandan	**To Pretend**	Neshan dadan
To Write	Neveshtan	**To Change**	Taaviz kardan
To Learn	Amokhtan	**I Can**	Man mitavanam
To Teach	Dars dadan	**To Return**	Pas dadan
To Take	Griftan	**To Borrow**	Gharz kardan
To Turn on	Roshan	**To Sit**	Nashastan
To Turn off	Khamosh	**To Need**	Ehtiyagh
To Close	Bastan	**To Say**	Goftan
To Put	Gozashtan	**To Remove**	Vardashtan
To Allow	Agazaeh	**To Travel**	Mosaferat kardan
To Lift	Boland	**To Eat**	Khordan
To Open	Baz kardan	**To Exchange**	Taaviz kardan
To Wish	Arzou	**To Mix**	Makhloot kardan
To Enter	Vared	**To Belong**	Motoaalegh bodan
To Come	Amadan	**To Feel**	Ehsase
To Move	Ja be ja	**To Stop**	Tavaghof
To Rent	Ajaraeh	**To Ask**	Khastan, porsidan
To Remember	Bekhoter	**To Answer**	Gavab dadan
To Check	Deghat	**To Decide**	Tasmim grafian
To Call	Sedozadan	**To Sell**	Forokhtan
To Resemble	Shabi boudan	**To Wait**	Moatal shodan

Building Bridges

I Can	Man mitzavanam
I Do	Man kardan
I Go	Man raftan
I Need	Man ehtiyagh
I Want	Man khostan
I See	Man didan
I Like	Man dost
I Say	Man goftan
I Talk	Man sohbat

Phrases:

I am on the way

Man Daram {I am} Miyam {way}

Are you cold outside?

Aya {are} shoma {you} sardetan {cold} sar kharej {outside}

For Farsi; grammar, pronunciation, accent, conjugation, and sentence structure are recommended but not required for non-Shakespearean speakers. Please note that when Farsi is spelled into English transliteration sometimes "ga" is pronounced as "ja".

Pashto

Afghanistan has two official languages, one of which is Pashto. The language is spoken by approximately 12 million people in the Middle East, though the vast majority is concentrated in Afghanistan. Despite the lack of any documentation, the language is known to have started in the Helmand and Kandahar provinces of the country. The other language of Afghanistan is Dari, which is actually more commonly used in the country among the government and other official organizations. Although the precise number is unknown, about 16-20 percent of Afghanistan speak Pashto while about 35 percent speak Dari.

Spoken in: Afghanistan and Pakistan

I	Ze
Me	Ze
My	Zmaa
Mine	Zmaa
His	De hagha
Him	Hegha
Her	De dee
Hers	De Heghi
He	De
She	Hegha
Us	Mung
Our	Zemung
With you	Staa sera
With You {Plural}	Staasu sera (dzhma'a)
With her	De Heghi sera
With him	De Heghe sera
With Them	De Heghuy sera
Without me	Ze me ne beghir
Without	Bee / beghir
Without you	Staa ne beghir
Without you {Plural}	Staasu ne beghir (dzhma'a)
Them, They	Heghu/ Duy
Their	De Heghuy/ De duy
You	Taa
You {Plural}	Taasu
I am	Ze yem
I was	Ze wem
I will	Ze be wukram
Are you	Aaye ta
We	Mung
Without her	De Heghi ne beghir
Without Them	De Heghuy ne beghir
Without Him	De Heghe ne beghir
With me	Zeme sere
For you	Staa de pera
To be	Kumaki fia'al
Yours	Staasu
We are	Munga
With us	Ze mung sera
Without us	Ze mung ne beghir
Who	Tsok

What	Tse	**Something**	Tse shay
If	Ke tsheeri	**Sometimes**	Kéla
Similar	Yawshaan	**Somewhere**	Biaa tsheerta
Where	Tshéeri	**Yes**	Bálee / ho
Were	Woo	**No**	Ne
When	Kela	**Less**	Kam
Only	Tenha	**Instead**	Pe bedel
Was	Woo	**Including**	Shamil
Other	Nor	**While**	Ter tsu tshi
Since	De / raasi	**Someone**	Yawtsok
Same	Yawshay	**Again**	Biaa
With	Sera	**Away**	Leri
Already	Pekhwa	**But**	Láakin
Together	Sera	**Don't**	Me kewa
Then	No	**Both**	Dwara
Than	Ter	**Because**	Dzéka tshi
More	Ddeer	**Still, Yet**	Laa
Very	Beekhi	**Time**	Dzal
Much, a lot	Ziyat	**Time**	Wakht
From	Ne	**Time**	Wakht / sa'st
And	Aw	**Also, Too**	Hum
Before	De mekha	**Around**	Nidzhi
After	Wrusta le	**Never**	Hítskela
Afterwards	Wrusta	**Of course**	Wáli ne
To	Te	**Here**	Dalee
The	Kmeki fia'al	**This**	Daa
That	Deghe	**OK**	Tteek
That	Tshi	**Just**	Saqhi
Is	Sta, shta	**Although**	Agar tshi
Which	Kum	**Through**	Pe zeri'a
For	De paara	**It is**	De day
Of	De	**Everywhere**	Her tshrta
Against	Khelaf	**Ready**	Tayaar
Always	Tel	**Soon**	Zar
Until	Póri / ter	**Except**	Bee le
Everything	Hártse	**Between**	Per mandz ki
Every	Har	**Now**	Os
Even If	Ke tse ham	**Later**	Wrusta
Things	Shayan	**Toward**	Khwate
There	Helta /delta	**How Much & How Many**	Tsomra
Into	Denena	**Neither**	Ne
Or	Aw	**None**	Hits
On	Ba'andi	**Nobody**	Hítsok
About	Pe baabat ki	**Maybe**	Shayad
How	Tsénga	**Way**	Lare
In	Ki (kssi)	**Why**	Wáli
Nothing	Hits	**Side**	Arrkh
At	Pe	**Everybody**	Hártsok
Almost	Taqriben	**A Few**	Yaw tso

Small	Werrúkey	**Name**	Num
Big	Loyína	**Last name**	Aakhiri num
Hot	Tod	**What is your name**	Sta num tse de
Cold	Yakh	**How old are you**	Sta umer tse de
Up	Porta	**Welcome**	Her kelay
Down	Ksséte	**Years**	Kaalone
Person	Seray	**Sky**	Aasman
People	Khalq, khaleg	**Night**	Shpa
Fast	Zher	**Light**	Ranna
Slow	Aa(h)ista	**Darkness**	Tiyare
Day	Wradz	**Morning**	Saqhaar
Tomorrow	Sabaa	**House**	Kor
Today	Nen	**Car**	Motter
Yesterday	Parun	**Left**	Kinnláas
Good	Khe	**Right**	Khailáas
Bad	Badláarey	**Place**	Dzaay
Hello	Her kelay	**Straight**	Naigh
Goodbye	Pe mekhe kha	**Parents**	Mor pelar
How are you	Tsenga yee	**Book**	Kitaab
Nice to meet you	Sta tse pe melawaidu khoshqháala shum	**Problem**	Keshela/ mesela
Good Night	Shpa de pe khair	**Behind**	Pasee
Good Afternoon	De gharmay salam	**Front**	Mekh
Good Morning	De seher salam	**Near**	Nizhdee
Friend	Dost	**Far**	Líri
Mom	Mor	**Sun**	Lmar
Dad	Pelar	**Better**	Bihtar
Brother	Wror	**Worse**	Bed
Sister	Khor	**Beautiful**	Sskéley
Cousin	Trorzay	**Real**	Asli
Grandfather	Baabaa	**Easy**	Aasan
Grandmother	Anaa	**Hard**	Kelek
Please	Mihrebani	**Next**	Aainda
Thank you	Teshakor	**One**	Yaw
Sorry	Be khana ghwarem	**Two**	Dwa
New	Neway	**Three**	Dray
Inside	Denena	**Four**	Tselor
Outside	Behar	**Five**	Pindze
Different	Bedal	**Six**	Shpazz
First	Aawal	**Seven**	Wa
Last	Aakhir	**Eight**	Aate
Child	Mashom/ betchi	**Nine**	Nehe
Man	Seray	**Ten**	Les
Women	Téni	**Number**	Shaire/ a'aded
Week	Awta	**Month**	Miaasht

To Talk	Khaberi kawel	**To Drive**	Tshelawel
To Walk	Gerdzedel	**To Pay**	Aada kewel
To Run	Dzghéledel	**To Buy**	Aghistel
To Sleep	Wede kidel	**To Practice**	Masheq kewel
To Begin	Shoru kewel	**To Prepare**	Aamaada kewel
To Finish	Khalaasawel	**To Meet**	Molaqaat kewel
To Drink	Tskhel	**To Fly**	Alwetel
To Smoke	Tskawem	**To Visit**	Molaqaat kewel
To Prefer	Terjih werkewel	**To Swim**	Awbaazi kewel
To Loose	Eele kewel	**To Show**	Sseyel
To Forget	Heerawel	**To Know**	Péezhenedaidel
To Hold	Saatel	**To Think**	Sotsh kewel
To Follow	Manel	**To Believe**	Yaqeen kewel
To Continue	Dzhaari saatel	**To Love**	Mayenidel
To Want	Ghokhtel	**To Like**	Khwakhwel
To Stay	Paatikaidel	**To Use**	Isti'maalewel
To Keep	Saatel	**To Try**	Koshesh kewel
To Play	Lobi kewel	**To Understand**	Pohéedel
To Get	Haasilewel	**To Have**	Larel
To Help	Meded kewel	**To Happen**	Paikhidel
To Go	Telel	**To Recognize**	Peezhend
To Give	Prekhewdel	**To Hear**	Awreedel
To Receive	Niwel	**To Listen**	Awreedel
To Bring	Raawelel	**To Press**	Drebwel
To Work	Káara kewel	**To Promise**	Wa'ade kewel
To Hope	Umayd kewel	**To Choose**	Khwa khewel
To Live	Ósedel	**To Arrive**	Raasidel
To Find	Múndel	**To Leave**	Prikhiwdel
To Look	Ketel	**To Leave**	Tsa prikhiwdel
To Search	Telaash kewel	**To Do**	Kewel
To See	Lidel	**To Order**	Qhukm kewel
To Read	Lwestel	**To Pretend**	Behaane kewel
To Write	Likel	**To Change**	Bedlewel
To Learn	Zda kewel	**I Can**	Ze shem
To Teach	Ders werkewl	**To Return**	We pesi kewel
To Take	Ághistel	**To Borrow**	Qered ighistel
To Turn on	Tshelaane wel	**To Sit**	Kinaastel
To Turn off	Bende wel	**To Need**	Daroret
To Close	Khalaasawel	**To Say**	Wáayel
To Put	Izzdel	**To Remove**	Deri kewel
To Allow	Idzhazet werkewel	**To Travel**	Sefer kewel
To Lift	Dzhegawel	**To Eat**	Khwrel
To Open	Biarte kewel	**To Exchange**	Tebaadila kewel
To Wish	Arzo kewel	**To Mix**	Kedwewl kewel
To Enter	Nenawetel	**To Belong**	Lerel
To Come	Reetelel	**To Feel**	Mehsos kewel
To Move	Khwedzidel	**To Stop**	Wedriadel
To Rent	Pe Keraaya werkewel	**To Ask**	Tepos kewel
To Remember	Yaad satel	**To Answer**	Dzheweb werkewel
To Check	Tshaar khaane kewel	**To Decide**	Fisele kewel
To Call	Raabólel	**To Sell**	Khersewel
To Resemble	Moshaabihet lerel	**To Wait**	Intizzer kewel

Building Bridges

I Can	Ze sham
I Do	Ze kewem
I Go	Ze zzam
I Need	Ze daroret lerem
I Want	Ze ghwáarrem
I See	Ze poheshom
I Like	Zmaa khwekha de
I Say	Ze wáayem
I Talk	Ze khaberi kawem

I want to go home
Zuh ghwaarum che Kor ze zza
I want that to home go

Go home!
Kor ze zza!
Home to go

Pronunciation, accents, grammar, and proper sentence structure are required for Pashto. For the Pashto language it's also recommended to learn how to pronounce the "kh" (refer back to introduction).

Chapter 3: Asian Languages

Section I: Sino-Tibetan Family (Chinese)

- Cantonese
- Mandarin

Cantonese

Spoken by the Chinese, Cantonese is certainly not a mainstream language to the culture. Although the official language of China is Mandarin, a vast amount of people speak Cantonese, most notable in the country's Southern areas. The language is also spoken off the mainland, specifically in Hong Kong. Cantonese is not a dialect of Mandarin, rather, it differs in its own unique written characters, vocabulary and grammar. The written form of Cantonese isn't used frequently, as is considered to be very casual and informal. Cantonese is also spoken throughout Europe, some parts of North America, New Zealand and Malaysia.

Spoken in: Southern China, Hong Kong, Macau, Malaysia, Singapore.

I	O
Me	O
My	Ote
Mine	Ote
His	Ta te
Him	Ta
Her	Ta
Hers	Tate
He	Ta
She	Ta
Us	Otai
Our	Otai
With you	Laei
With You {Plural}	Wolae, tan laei
With her	Wolae, tan laei
With him	Wota
With Them	Wota
Without me	Wotamon
Without	Motyao
Without you	Motyao laei
Without you {Plural}	Mot yao laei
Them, They	Tamon
Their	Coyitaei
You	Laei
You {Plural}	Laei
I am	O hay
I was	
I will	
Are you	Laei
We	Ote
Without her	Motyao ta
Without Them	Motyao tamon
Without Him	Motyao ta
With me	Ton o
For you	Bay lay
To be	Jom wi
Yours	Laei tai
We are	Otai hay
With us	Tom otai
Without us	Mo o tai
Who	Pinko

What	Ma yae	**Something**	Yati yae
If	Yugo	**Sometimes**	Yau si
Similar	Sontzi	**Somewhere**	Yau to
Where	Pindo	**Yes**	Hai
Were	Hay	**No**	m-hai
When	Gaisi	**Less**	Yatii
Only	Gi yaou	**Instead**	
Was	Hay	**Including**	Pao kut
Other	Da-i-ti	**While**	Yatan
Since	Gi-chan	**Someone**	Yao koi yan
Same	Surnton	**Again**	Toi ti
With	Ton	**Away**	Lai hoi
Already	Igen	**But**	Tan hai
Together	Yazai	**Don't**	m-ho
Then	Yitin	**Both**	Aun ko
Than	Co	**Because**	Yang wy
More	Toti	**Still, Yet**	Yang yin
Very	Mton	**Time**	Tzi
Much, a lot	Toti	**Time**	Hai ko s
From	Yaou	**Time**	Jon
And	Who, ton	**Also, Too**	Do hai
Before	Ichin	**Around**	Pa wy
After	Gee hou	**Never**	Wing yang
Afterwards	Gee-hou	**Of course**	Tong ying
To	Hoy	**Here**	Jeloy
The	Ligo	**This**	Niko
That	Igo	**OK**	Ok
That		**Just**	Amam
Is	Hay	**Although**	Soy yin
Which	Binko	**Through**	Chin go
For	Wy, bai	**It is**	I-go-hai
Of		**Everywhere**	Ja wy
Against	Dai-kon	**Ready**	Jam pay ho
Always	Si sheung	**Soon**	Chou-fai
Until	Jek chi	**Except**	Jip-saou
Everything	Chimpo	**Between**	Jon-kan
Every	Moi ko	**Now**	Yi-ga
Even If	Samgi igo	**Later**	Gee-hou
Things		**Toward**	Iipin
There	Go tow	**How Much & How Many**	Gaiito
Into	Ya tae	**Neither**	Mo
Or	Wak- jae	**None**	Mo yae
On	Ha-y	**Nobody**	Mo yon
About	Cha am do	**Maybe**	Wa che
How	Dim yae	**Way**	Ni pin
In	Ya pin	**Why**	Tim gai
Nothing	Mo yae	**Side**	Pin
At		**Everybody**	Moi go yon
Almost	Cham do	**A Few**	Yatii

164

Small	Sai	**Name**	Maen, singman
Big	Tai	**Last name**	Sing
Hot	Yit	**What is your name**	Lai ko maen
Cold	Ton	**How old are you**	Lai kai soy
Up	Sam	**Welcome**	Fon yen
Down	Ha	**Years**	Lin
Person	Yan	**Sky**	Tinn
People	Yan	**Night**	Yeman
Fast	Fai	**Light**	Tang
Slow	Man	**Darkness**	Yeman
Day	Koi day	**Morning**	Jo sahue
Tomorrow	Tinya	**House**	Ohh
Today	Kam yap	**Car**	Che
Yesterday	Kam ya	**Left**	Jo
Good	Ho	**Right**	Yao
Bad	Mo	**Place**	Day fon
Hello	Wy	**Straight**	Tze
Goodbye	Bai bai	**Parents**	Fumo
How are you	Ne ho ma	**Book**	Su
Nice to meet you	Han woi	**Problem**	Quanan
Good Night	Jo tao	**Behind**	Hao min
Good Afternoon	M on	**Front**	Tinmin
Good Morning	Jo san	**Near**	Kan
Friend	Pang yao	**Far**	Yuen
Mom	Mom	**Sun**	Tayo
Dad	Papa	**Better**	Hali
Brother	Coco	**Worse**	Soi di
Sister	Kate	**Beautiful**	Lang, mai lai
Cousin	Pio	**Real**	Chan
Grandfather	Jo fo	**Easy**	Yong yi
Grandmother	Jo mo	**Hard**	Lan
Please	M goi	**Next**	Hago
Thank you	Totze	**One**	Ya
Sorry	Toi-m-ji	**Two**	Laon go
New	San	**Three**	Sam
Inside	Yap in	**Four**	Sae
Outside	Cho pin	**Five**	M
Different	M ton	**Six**	Lo
First	Taya	**Seven**	Tza
Last	Joi hao	**Eight**	Ba
Child	Sai low	**Nine**	Kao
Man	Nam yan	**Ten**	Sa
Women	No yan	**Number**	Somo
Week	Otae	**Month**	Yuu

To Talk	Kon	**To Drive**	Tza
To Walk	Han	**To Pay**	Paii
To Run	Tzao	**To Buy**	Maii
To Sleep	Fan kao	**To Practice**	Ho tza
To Begin	Hoi tzi	**To Prepare**	Jon pui
To Finish	Yin	**To Meet**	Kin min
To Drink	Yam	**To Fly**	Fai
To Smoke	Sae yin	**To Visit**	Tam
To Prefer		**To Swim**	Yao soi
To Loose	Siu	**To Show**	Taii
To Forget	Monkai	**To Know**	Tido
To Hold	Jaji	**To Think**	San
To Follow	Kan ji	**To Believe**	San sun
To Continue	Kai jo	**To Love**	Hoy
To Want	Son	**To Like**	Tom ghi
To Stay	Lao ji	**To Use**	Yon
To Keep	Ja ji	**To Try**	Si
To Play	Wan	**To Understand**	Min pa
To Get	Lo	**To Have**	Yauu
To Help	Pon	**To Happen**	Pasan
To Go	Hoi	**To Recognize**	Lang ba
To Give	Fai	**To Hear**	Taen
To Receive	Sao	**To Listen**	Taen
To Bring	Tai	**To Press**	Kam
To Work	Kunzo	**To Promise**	Ta yang
To Hope	Hai mo	**To Choose**	Kaan
To Live	Ji	**To Arrive**	To da
To Find	Wan	**To Leave**	Lai hoy
To Look	Tai	**To Leave** {Something}	Laou tai
To Search	Wan	**To Do**	Jo
To See	Tai	**To Order**	Ten
To Read	Tuo	**To Pretend**	Tza tai
To Write	Se	**To Change**	Wun
To Learn	H*o*	**I Can** {no infinitive}	O lan gao
To Teach	Kao	**To Return**	Toi woi
To Take	Lo	**To Borrow**	Tze
To Turn on	Hoi	**To Sit**	Tzo tai
To Turn off	San	**To Need**	Soy yau
To Close	San	**To Say**	Kon
To Put	Bai	**To Remove**	Lik hoi
To Allow	Yong hai	**To Travel**	Loi yao
To Lift	Ling hai	**To Eat**	Se
To Open	Hoi	**To Exchange**	Wun
To Wish	Hay mo	**To Mix**	Lo mai
To Enter	Yap hoi	**To Belong**	So i
To Come	Lai	**To Feel**	Tam ko
To Move	Yo	**To Stop**	Tang
To Rent	Jo	**To Ask**	Man
To Remember	Kaiji	**To Answer**	Ta
To Check	Cha	**To Decide**	Kui ten
To Call	Gyo	**To Sell**	Mai
To Resemble	Tzi	**To Wait**	Tang

Building Bridges

I Can	O lan gao
I Do	
I Go	Oi
I Need	O soy yiu
I Want	O son
I See	O toi do
I Like	O ton yi
I Say	O kon
I Talk	O kon

I want to go to your house

O son hoy laei tai ohh

O {I} son {want} hoi {go} laei – tai {your} ohh {house}

I want to leave you there

O son lau tai laei go tow

O {I} son {want} laou- tai {to leave} laei {your} go tow {there}

For Cantonese; grammar, sentence structure, pronunciation, and accent are required for Shakespearean and non-Shakespearean speakers.

Mandarin

Mandarin is the most commonly spoken language in the world. It is the official language of China (the most populated country in the world) and Taiwan. However, most people call the language "Chinese." Still, because of the greater division of Old Chinese and Middle Chinese, there are many dialects of the language which spread throughout China and its neighboring nations. It is spoken in Hong Kong and is becoming more popular, though Cantonese is still the more dominant language. In China, children are taught Mandarin throughout their education, though local languages are taught in addition in Taiwan.

Spoken in: China (the People's Republic of China and the Republic of China), Singapore.

I	Wo
Me	Wo
My	Wo de
Mine	Wo de
His	Ta de
Him	Ta
Her	Ta
Hers	Ta de
He	Ta
She	Ta
Us	Wo men
Our	Wo men de
With you	Tong ni
With You {Plural}	Tong ni men
With her	Tong ta
With him	Tong ta
With Them	Tong ta men
Without me	Bu yao wo
Without	Bu yao
Without you	Bu yao ni
Without you {Plural}	Bu yao ni men
Them, They	Ta men
Their	Ta men de
You	Ni
You {Plural}	Ni men
I am	Wo shi
I was	Wo guo qu shi
I will	Wo jiang yao
Are you	Ni shi bu shi
We	Wo men
Without her	Bu yao ta
Without Them	Bu yao ta men
Without Him	Bu yao ta
With me	Tong wo
For you	Wei le ni
To be	(not used)
Yours	Ni de
We are	Women shi
With us	Tong wo men
Without us	Mei you wo men
Who	Shei

What	Shen me	**Something**	Yi xie dong xi
If	Ru guo	**Sometimes**	You shi
Similar	Xiang yi de	**Somewhere**	Mou chu
Where	Na li	**Yes**	Shi, dui
Were	Shi	**No**	Bu
When	Shen me shi hou	**Less**	Gen shao
Only	Zhi	**Instead**	Dai ti
Was	Shi	**Including**	Bao kou
Other	Bu tong de	**While**	---de shi hou
Since	Zi cong---yi hou	**Someone**	You ren
Same	Tong yang	**Again**	Zai lai
With	Tong	**Away**	Bu zai
Already	Yi jing	**But**	Dan shi
Together	Zai yi qi	**Don't**	Bu yao
Then	Jie guo	**Both**	Liang ge
Than	Bi jiao	**Because**	Ying wei
More	Geng	**Still, Yet**	Dao xian zai
Very	Hen, tai	**Time**	Shi
Much, a lot	Hen duo	**Time**	Shi jian
From	Cong	**Time**	Zhong tou
And	Tong ji	**Also, Too**	Ye
Before	Zhi qian	**Around**	
After	Yi hou	**Never**	Cong lai bu
Afterwards	Hou lai	**Of course**	Dang ran
To	Dao	**Here**	Zhei li
The	(not used)	**This**	Zhe ge
That	Zhe ge	**OK**	Hao le, ke yi
That		**Just**	Qia hao
Is	Shi	**Although**	Sui ran
Which	Shen me ?	**Through**	
For	Wei le	**It is**	Zhe shi
Of	De	**Everywhere**	Dao chu
Against	Dui zhe	**Ready**	Zhun bei le
Always	Zong shi	**Soon**	Zao
Until	Zhi dao----cai	**Except**	Chu le---yi wai
Everything	Mei yang dong xi	**Between**	Zhi jian
Every	Mei	**Now**	Xian zai
Even If	Ji shi	**Later**	Hou lai
Things	Dong xi	**Toward**	Wang
There	Na bian	**How Much & How Many**	Duo shao
Into	Jin ru	**Neither**	Ji bu----you bu
Or	Hai shi	**None**	Mei you
On	Zai	**Nobody**	Mei ren
About	Guan yu	**Maybe**	Ye xu
How	Zen me yang	**Way**	(what way?)
In	Zai ---nei	**Why**	Wei shen me?
Nothing	Mei you ren he	**Side**	Bian
At	zai	**Everyone**	Mei yi ge ren
Almost	Cha bu duo	**A Few**	Ji ge

Small	Xiao	**Name**	Ming zi
Big	Da	**Last name**	Xin
Hot	Re	**What is you name**	Ni xin shen me
Cold	Neng	**How old are you**	Ni you ji sui
Up	Shang	**Welcome**	Huan ying
Down	Xia	**Years**	(what year?)
Person	Ren	**Sky**	Tian
People	Ren (men)	**Night**	Ye wan
Fast	Kuai	**Light**	Guang
Slow	Man	**Darkness**	He an
Day	Ri, tian	**Morning**	Zao chen
Tomorrow	Ming tian	**House**	Fang zi
Today	Jin tian	**Car**	Che zi
Yesterday	Zuo tian	**Left**	Zuo bian
Good	Hao	**Right**	You bian
Bad	Bu hao	**Place**	Di fang
Hello	Ni hao	**Straight**	Yi zhi
Goodbye	Zai jian	**Parents**	Fu mu
How are you	Ni hao bu hao	**Book**	Shu
Nice to meet you	(not used)	**Problem**	Wen ti
Good Night	Wan an	**Behind**	Hou bian
Good Afternoon	(not used)	**Front**	Qian bian
Good Morning	Zao	**Near**	Fu jing
Friend	Peng you	**Far**	Yuan
Mom	Ma	**Sun**	Tai yang
Dad	De	**Better**	Geng hao
Brother	Xiong di	**Worse**	Geng bu hao
Sister	Jie mei	**Beautiful**	Mei, piao liang
Cousin	Biao zi mei	**Real**	Zhen de
Grandfather	Zu fu	**Easy**	Yong yi
Grandmother	Zu mu	**Hard**	Ma fang
Please	Qing	**Next**	Xia yi ge
Thank you	Xie xie	**One**	Yi
Sorry	Dui bi qi	**Two**	Er, liang
New	Xin	**Three**	San
Inside	Zai nei	**Four**	Shi
Outside	Zai wai	**Five**	Wu
Different	Bu yi yang	**Six**	Liu
First	Di yi	**Seven**	Qi
Last	Zui hou	**Eight**	Ba
Child	Hai zi	**Nine**	Jiu
Man	Nan ren	**Ten**	Shi
Women	Nuu ren	**Number**	Shu mu
Week	xing qi, li bai	**Month**	Yue

To Talk	Jiang hua	**To Drive**	Kai (che)
To Walk	Zuo lu	**To Pay**	Fu qian
To Run	Pao	**To Buy**	Mai
To Sleep	Shui jiao	**To Practice**	Lian xi
To Begin	Kai shi	**To Prepare**	Zhun bei
To Finish	Wan cheng	**To Meet**	Hui jian
To Drink	He	**To Fly**	Fei
To Smoke	Chou yan	**To Visit**	Bai fang
To Prefer	Ning yuan	**To Swim**	You yun
To Loose	Diu shi	**To Show**	Biao shi
To Forget	Wang ji	**To Know**	Zhi dao
To Hold	Na	**To Think**	Xiang
To Follow	Gen zhe	**To Believe**	Xiang xin
To Continue	Ji xu	**To Love**	Ai
To Want	Xiang yao	**To Like**	Xi huan
To Stay	Liu xia	**To Use**	Yong
To Keep	Bao cun	**To Try**	Shi yi shi
To Play	Wan	**To Understand**	Dong, ming bai
To Get	De	**To Have**	You
To Help	Bang mang	**To Happen**	Fa sheng
To Go	Zou	**To Recognize**	Ren shi
To Give	Gei	**To Hear**	Ting
To Receive	Shou	**To Listen**	Ting dao
To Bring	Dai lai	**To Press**	Ya
To Work	Zuo gong	**To Promise**	Da ying
To Hope	Xi wang	**To Choose**	Xuan ze
To Live	Sheng huo	**To Arrive**	Da dao
To Find	Zhao dao	**To Leave**	Li kai
To Look	Kan, wang	**To Leave {Something}**	Liu xia
To Search	Zhao	**To Do**	Zuo
To See	Kan	**To Order**	Ding
To Read	Duo	**To Pretend**	Zuang zuo
To Write	Xie	**To Change**	Huan
To Learn	Xue	**I Can**	Wo ke yi
To Teach	Jiao	**To Return**	Huan
To Take	Na	**To Borrow**	Jie
To Turn on	Kai	**To Sit**	Zuo
To Turn off	Guan	**To Need**	Xu yao
To Close	Guan diao	**To Say**	Shuo
To Put	Fang	**To Remove**	La diao
To Allow	Yun xu	**To Travel**	Luu you
To Lift	Tai	**To Eat**	Chi
To Open	Da kai	**To Exchange**	Dui huan
To Wish	Zhu, xi wang	**To Mix**	Hun huo
To Enter	Jin qu	**To Belong**	Shu yu
To Come	Lai	**To Feel**	Gan jue
To Move	Dong	**To Stop**	Ting zi
To Rent	Zu	**To Ask**	Wen
To Remember	Ji dao	**To Answer**	Hui da
To Check	Jian cha	**To Decide**	Jue ding
To Call	Jiao	**To Sell**	Mai
To Resemble	Xiang	**To Wait**	Deng

Building Bridges

I Can	wo ko-yi
I Do	wo zuo
I Go	wo qu
I Need	wo xu-yao
I Want	wo yao
I See	wo kan
I Like	wo xi-huan
I Say	wo shuo
I Talk	wo jiang

The spoken Chinese language is rather easy to learn, because there is almost no grammar to study, no conjugation nor declination not even female or male to remember. But there are other difficulties since the pronunciation of so many words with different meanings is in most cases almost the same, therefore they cannot use an alphabet, but each word has his own character. Most meanings are expressed by two or more words or in the written language by characters or symbols if you like. Another difficult aspect for foreigners is the fact that there are no subordinate clauses like in European languages. The word order of a sentence has to be changed entirely, mostly beginning from the end. For example:

The house, which I like, is too small.
I like (of) house, too small (Without is)
Wo xi-huan de fang-zi tai xiao

My brother, who is in England, speaks Chinese
My in England (of) brother speak Chinese
Wo-de zai ying-guo de xiong-di jiang zhong-wen

For Mandarin; grammar, sentence structure, pronunciation, and accent are required for Shakespearean and non-Shakespearean speakers.

Asian Languages

Section II: Japonic
- Japanese

Japanese

Japanese is a complex language, marked with accents and pitch signals. It was developed from various influences, including kanji, alphabet characters derived from China as well as hiragana and katakana, which are syllabic characters. Japanese takes its main inspirations from the Chinese language and English, as traditional Arabic numbers are used. Though this is frequent, the Japanese do not completely abandon their native numerical characters, as they are common as well. Over 127 million people worldwide speak Japanese, and the vast majority of them live in Japan. However, when Japan invaded countries in the Western Hemisphere like the Pacific Islands, Korea and Taiwan, Japanese soldiers forced the natives to convert to their language. To this day, many people in those areas still speak Japanese.

Spoken in: Japan

I	Watashi wa
Me	Watashi ni
My	Watashi no
Mine	Watashi no
His	Kare no
Him	Kare ni
Her	Kanojo no
Hers	Kanojo no
He	Kare wa
She	Kanojo wa
Us	Watashi tachi ni
Our	Watashi tachi no
With you	Anata to
With You {Plural}	Anata ni
With her	Kanojo to
With him	Kare to
With Them	Karera to
Without me	Watashi nashi de
Without	Nash de
Without you	Anata nashi de
Without you {Plural}	Anata nashi ni
Them, They	Karera ni, karera wa
Their	Karera no
You	Anata
You {Plural}	Anata wa
I am	Desu
I was	Watashiwa desu
I will	Watashiw desho
Are you	Anata wa
We	Watashi tachi
Without her	Kanajo nashide
Without Them	Karera nashide
Without Him	Kare nashide
With me	Watashi to
For you	Anatano tameni
To be	Naru
Yours	Anata no
We are	Watashitachi w a desu
With us	Watashitachi to
Without us	Watashitachi nashide
Who	Dare

What	Nani	Something	Nanika
If	Moshimo	Sometimes	Tokidoki
Similar	Ni	Somewhere	Dokoka de
Where	Doko	Yes	Hai
Were		No	Iie
When	Itsu	Less	Sukunai
Only	Dake	Instead	Kawari ni
Was	Naze	Including	Komi
Other	Hoka no	While	Aida
Since	Irai	Someone	Dareha
Same	Onaji	Again	Mata
With	To	Away	Hou hou
Already	Sudeni	But	Shihaski
Together	Issho ni	Don't	Suruna
Then	Skono kara	Both	Ryoho
Than	Yori	Because	Kara, No tame
More	Motto	Still, Yet	Mada
Very	Totemo	Time	Kai
Much, a lot	Taksan	Time	Toki
From	Kara	Time	Jikan
And	To	Also, Too	Mata, sugiru
Before	Mae	Around	Mawatte, mawaru
After	No ato	Never	Keshite
Afterwards	To iu koto wa	Of course	Mochiron
To	E	Here	Koko
The		This	Kore wa
That	Are, sore	OK	Ookee
That		Just	Chodo
Is	Desu	Although	
Which	Dochira	Through	Toshite
For	Tameni	It is	Desu
Of	No	Everywhere	Doko nidemo
Against	Hamtai no	Ready	Yoiga dekiru
Always	Itsumo	Soon	Sugu
Until	Made	Except	
Everything	Subete	Between	Kara
Every	Subete no	Now	Ima
Even If	Moshi derae	Later	Atode
Things	Mo mo	Toward	Sotte
There	Soko, sochira	How Much & How Many	Ikura, iktsu, ikutsu
Into	Nakani	Neither	
Or	Matawa	None	Nashi
On	Veni	Nobody	Daremo
About	Tsuite	Maybe	Moshka shtara
How	Nan de	Way	Hou how
In	Ni	Why	Naze
Nothing	Nanimo nai	Side	Soba
At	De	Everybody	Minna
Almost	Hotondo	A Few	Skoshi

Small	Chiisai	**Name**	Namae
Big	Ookii	**Last name**	See
Hot	Atsui	**What is your name**	O namae wa
Cold	Tsumetai	**How old are you**	Nan sai
Up	Ue	**Welcome**	Yokoso
Down	Shita	**Years**	Nen
Person	Hito	**Sky**	Sora
People	Hito	**Night**	Yoru
Fast	Susumu	**Light**	Usui
Slow	Osoi	**Darkness**	Kurai
Day	Nichi	**Morning**	Asa
Tomorrow	Ashta	**House**	Ie
Today	Kyoo	**Car**	Kuruma
Yesterday	Kinoo	**Left**	Hidari
Good	Oishii	**Right**	Migi
Bad	Warui	**Place**	Basho
Hello	Ko nichi wa	**Straight**	Massugu
Goodbye	Sayonara	**Parents**	Rooshin
How are you	O genki desu ka	**Book**	Hon
Nice to meet you		**Problem**	Hondai
Good Night	Oyasumi nasai	**Behind**	Ushiro
Good Afternoon	Kon nichi wa	**Front**	No mae
Good Morning	Ohayoo gozaimas	**Near**	Chikaku
Friend	Tomodachi	**Far**	Tooi
Mom	O ka san	**Sun**	Taiyo
Dad	O to san	**Better**	Motto ii
Brother	Ani, otooto	**Worse**	Motto warui
Sister	Ane, imoto	**Beautiful**	Utsukushii
Cousin	Itoko	**Real**	Honmono
Grandfather	Ojii san	**Easy**	Kantan
Grandmother	O ba san	**Hard**	Muzukashii
Please	Onegai shimas	**Next**	Tsugi
Thank you	Arigatoo	**One**	Iich
Sorry	Gomen nasai	**Two**	Nee
New	Atarashii	**Three**	San
Inside	Naka	**Four**	Shee
Outside	Soto	**Five**	Go
Different	Chigau	**Six**	Loko
First	Saisho, ichiban	**Seven**	Sichi
Last	Saigo	**Eight**	Hachi
Child	Kodomo	**Nine**	Koo
Man	Otoko	**Ten**	Niju
Women	Onna	**Number**	Bangoo
Week	Shuu	**Month**	Tsuki

To Talk	Hanasu	**To Drive**	Unten suru
To Walk	Aruku	**To Pay**	Harau
To Run	Hashiru	**To Buy**	Kau
To Sleep	Nemuru	**To Practice**	Renshu
To Begin	Hajimeru	**To Prepare**	Yoi
To Finish	Owaru	**To Meet**	Machiawaseru
To Drink	Nomu	**To Fly**	Tobu
To Smoke	Tabako o suu	**To Visit**	Mimau
To Prefer	No haca yo	**To Swim**	Oyogu
To Loose	Yurui	**To Show**	Miseru
To Forget	Wasureru	**To Know**	Shiru
To Hold	Matsu	**To Think**	Kangaeru
To Follow	Shitagau	**To Believe**	Shinzuru
To Continue	Tuzukeru	**To Love**	Aisuku
To Want	Hoshii	**To Like**	Suki
To Stay	Tomaru	**To Use**	Tsukau
To Keep	Hojisuru	**To Try**	Tamesu
To Play	Suru	**To Understand**	Wakaru
To Get	Noru	**To Have**	Aru
To Help	Tetsudau	**To Happen**	Okoru
To Go	Iku	**To Recognize**	Wakaru
To Give	Ageru	**To Hear**	Kiku
To Receive	Uketoru	**To Listen**	Kiku
To Bring	Hakobu	**To Press**	Airon o kakeru
To Work	Tsukau	**To Promise**	Yahusoku
To Hope	Nozomn	**To Choose**	Erabu
To Live	Sumu	**To Arrive**	Toochaku suru
To Find	Mituskeru	**To Leave**	Iku
To Look	Miru	**To Leave {Something}**	Saru
To Search	Sagas	**To Do**	Suru
To See	Miru	**To Order**	Chuumon suru
To Read	Yomu	**To Pretend**	Furi
To Write	Kaku	**To Change**	Kaeru
To Learn	Narau	**I Can**	Dehiru
To Teach	Oshieru	**To Return**	Kaeru
To Take	Hakob	**To Borrow**	Kariru
To Turn on	Tsukeru	**To Sit**	Suwara
To Turn off	Kesu	**To Need**	Iru
To Close	Shimaru	**To Say**	Iu
To Put	Oku	**To Remove**	Tori nozoku
To Allow		**To Travel**	Ryoko
To Lift	Mochiageru	**To Eat**	Taberu
To Open	Aku	**To Exchange**	Torikaeru
To Wish	Nozomu	**To Mix**	Mazeru
To Enter	Hairu	**To Belong**	Tsurete kuru
To Come	Kuru	**To Feel**	Kanzuru
To Move	Ugoku	**To Stop**	Tomaru
To Rent	Kariru	**To Ask**	Taguneru
To Remember	Oboeru, omoi dasu	**To Answer**	Kotaeru
To Check		**To Decide**	Kimeru
To Call	Yobu	**To Sell**	Uru
To Resemble		**To Wait**	Matsu

Building Bridges

I Can	Watashiwa dekiru
I Do	Watashiwa suru
I Go	Watashiwa iku
I Need	Watashiwa hitsuyo
I Want	Watashiwa hoshii
I See	Watashiwa miru
I Like	Watachiwa suki
I Say	Watachiwa iu
I Talk	Watachiwa hamasu

For the Japanese language; grammar, sentence structure, pronunciation, and accent are required for Shakespearean and non-Shakespearean speakers.

Asian Languages

Section III: Indo Aryan Languages
- Hindi
- Urdu

Hindi

Hindi was the first official language of India, though it is predominately spoken in the country's Central and Northern regions. Over time, India resolved to not have an official language, but rather to have various regions with official languages. Another Indian official language is Urdu, which is often mistaken for Hindi and vice versa because of their similarities. With its Arabic roots, Hindi was influenced from ancient Muslim armies, which inhabited the area under the Mughal Empire. Not many countries actually speak Hindi. So, it is only the fifth most common language in the world because of India's large population.

Spoken in: India, Pakistan Nepal, Kashmir, and Bangladesh

Are you	Tum kia
For you	Tumare Lye
He	Larka
Her	Wou
Hers	Larki
Him	Ye
His	Iska
I	Main
I am	Main hoon
I was	Main tha
I will	Karunga
Me	Main
Mine	Mera
My	Mera
Our	Tum
She	Larki
Their	Inka
Them, They	Ye'n
To be	Honewala
Us	Humara
We	Hum
We are	Hum Hain
Who	Kaun
With her	Ugke saath
With him	Inke saath
With me	Mere Saath
With Them	Inke saath
With us	Humare Saath
With you	Tumhane saath
With You {Plural}	Ugke saath
Without	Bina
Without her	Uske Bina
Without Him	Iske Bina
Without me	Mere Bina
Without Them	Inke Bina
Without us	Humare Bina
Without you	Tumare Bina
Without you {Plural}	Tumare Bina
You	Tum
You {Plural}	Tum
Yours	Tumahara

What	Kia	**Something**	Kuch
If	Agar	**Sometimes**	Kabhi kabhi
Similar	Milta	**Somewhere**	Kahin
Where	Kahaan	**Yes**	Haan
Were	Hum	**No**	Nahi
When	Kab	**Less**	Kaam
Only	Sirf	**Instead**	Bajai
Was	Tha	**Including**	Sab milake
Other	Aur	**While**	Us doran
Since	Smce	**Someone**	Koi
Same	Ek jaisa	**Again**	Wapis
With	Is	**Away**	Janaa
Already	Phele se	**But**	Kiu
Together	Saath	**Don't**	Nahi
Then	Pher	**Both**	Dono
Than	Phir	**Because**	Isle
More	Aur	**Still, Yet**	Abhi tak
Very	Bohut	**Time**	Waat
Much, a lot	Bohut	**Time**	Us waat
From	Jagaa	**Time**	Waat
And	Aur	**Also, Too**	Phir bhi
Before	Pehle	**Around**	Charo tarat
After	Bad	**Never**	Kabhi nahi
Afterwards	Bad main	**Of course**	Zahiri baat hai
To		**Here**	Idher
The		**This**	Yeh
That	Yeh	**OK**	Ok, theek hai
That		**Just**	Bus
Is		**Although**	
Which	Kaun sa	**Through**	Paas
For		**It is**	Hai
Of		**Everywhere**	Her Jagaa
Against	Khilaf	**Ready**	Taryar
Always	Hamesha	**Soon**	Jald
Until	Tab tak	**Except**	Manzoor
Everything	Sab kuch	**Between**	Dermiyan
Every	Her ek	**Now**	Abhi
Even If	Agar phir	**Later**	Bad main
Things	Cheez	**Toward**	Samne
There	Udhar	**How Much & How Many**	Kitne kaa, kitna our
Into		**Neither**	
Or	Or	**None**	Kuch nahi
On	Upar	**Nobody**	Koi nahi
About		**Maybe**	Shyed
How	Kaisa	**Way**	Raasta
In	Under	**Why**	Kiyu
Nothing	Kuch nahi	**Side**	Side
At		**Everybody**	Her Koi
Almost	Almost	**A Few**	kuch

Small	Chotta	**Name**	Nam
Big	Bara	**Last name**	Sir name
Hot	Garam	**What is your name**	Kia naam hai tumhara
Cold	Tanda	**How old are you**	Kitne saal kai ho
Up	Upar	**Welcome**	Namaaste
Down	Neeche	**Years**	Saal
Person	Insaan	**Sky**	Asmaan
People	Log	**Night**	Raath
Fast	Tez	**Light**	Roshni
Slow	Halka	**Darkness**	Andhera
Day	Din	**Morning**	Subha
Tomorrow	Kaal	**House**	Gihar
Today	Aaj	**Car**	Gari
Yesterday	Kaal	**Left**	Ulta
Good	Acha	**Right**	Seedha
Bad	Bura	**Place**	Jagaa
Hello	Saalam	**Straight**	Seedha
Goodbye	Khuda hafiz	**Parents**	Ma baap
How are you	Kaisse ho	**Book**	Kitab
Nice to meet you	Milke khushi	**Problem**	Mushkil
Good Night	Sojao	**Behind**	Peeche
Good Afternoon	Acha din	**Front**	Age
Good Morning	Acha din	**Near**	Kareeb
Friend	Dost	**Far**	Dur
Mom	Ma	**Sun**	Sooraj
Dad	Baap	**Better**	Behtar
Brother	Bhai	**Worse**	Batar
Sister	Behen	**Beautiful**	Khobsurat
Cousin	Rishtedar	**Real**	Asli
Grandfather	Dada	**Easy**	Ahsaan
Grandmother	Dadi	**Hard**	Mushkil
Please	Krip ya	**Next**	Agla
Thank you	Dhan ya vad	**One**	Ek
Sorry	Maafi	**Two**	Do
New	Nayi	**Three**	Teen
Inside	Under	**Four**	Char
Outside	Bahar	**Five**	Panch
Different	Hatke	**Six**	Chey
First	Pehla	**Seven**	Saat
Last	Akhri	**Eight**	Aant
Child	Bacha	**Nine**	Nau
Man	Mard	**Ten**	Dus
Women	Aurat	**Number**	Ginty
Week	Hafta	**Month**	Mahina

To Talk	Bolo na	**To Drive**	Chalana
To Walk	Chalaa	**To Pay**	Pagar dena
To Run	Bhago na	**To Buy**	Karidna
To Sleep	So na	**To Practice**	Practice kama
To Begin	Shuru karo	**To Prepare**	Teryari karna
To Finish	Khatam karo	**To Meet**	Milna
To Drink	Piyo na	**To Fly**	Urna
To Smoke	Piyo na	**To Visit**	Milna
To Prefer		**To Swim**	Terna
To Loose	Dheela rathna	**To Show**	Dikhana
To Forget	Bhulnana	**To Know**	Janaa
To Hold	Pakarna	**To Think**	Sochna
To Follow	Peecha karna	**To Believe**	Yakeen karna
To Continue	Begam na	**To Love**	Pyar karna
To Want	Chaye na	**To Like**	Pasand karna
To Stay	Rukgana	**To Use**	Istimal karna
To Keep	Pakro na	**To Try**	Koshish karna
To Play	Khelo	**To Understand**	Samaj na
To Get	Lena	**To Have**	Panaa
To Help	Madat karna	**To Happen**	Hone walaa
To Go	Chale jana	**To Recognize**	Phchchanaa
To Give	Dedena	**To Hear**	Suna
To Receive	Mangliena	**To Listen**	Suna
To Bring	Lana	**To Press**	Dabanaa
To Work	Kamkarna	**To Promise**	Wada karna
To Hope	Dua	**To Choose**	Pasand karna
To Live	Jheena	**To Arrive**	Poch jana
To Find	Dhundna	**To Leave**	Chale jana
To Look	Dhekna	**To Leave {Something}**	Chale jana
To Search	Dhunduna	**To Do**	Karna
To See	Dhekna	**To Order**	Hukum chalana
To Read	Parna	**To Pretend**	
To Write	Likhna	**To Change**	Badal na
To Learn	Seekna	**I Can**	Main karu
To Teach	Sikhana	**To Return**	Lotna
To Take	Lena	**To Borrow**	Udhar
To Turn on	Jhalana	**To Sit**	Bhetna
To Turn off	Bhuiana	**To Need**	Zaroorat
To Close	Bandkarna	**To Say**	Utha na
To Put	Rakhna	**To Remove**	Hatha dena
To Allow	Ijezat dena	**To Travel**	Safar karna
To Lift	Utha lena	**To Eat**	Khana
To Open	Chol na	**To Exchange**	Badal na
To Wish	Dua karna	**To Mix**	Milana
To Enter	Gihusna	**To Belong**	
To Come	Ajana	**To Feel**	Mehsoos kama
To Move	Hilna	**To Stop**	Rukh na
To Rent	Kiraya	**To Ask**	Puch na
To Remember	Yaad rakna	**To Answer**	Jawab dena
To Check	Check karna	**To Decide**	Te karna
To Call	Bulana	**To Sell**	Bech na
To Resemble	Milana	**To Wait**	Intizar karna

Building bridges

I Can	Maji karu hai
I Do	Maji Karna hai
I Go	Maji Chale jana
I Need	Maji Zaroorat
I Want	Maji Chaye na
I See	Maji Shekna hai
I Like	Maji Pasand karna bola
I Say	Maji Utha na
I Talk	Maji Bolo na

Phrases:

Where's the book

Kitab {book} ka haan {where} hain

How much does this cost

Yeh {this} kitne ka {how much} hai {cost}

For the Hindi language; grammar, pronunciation, accent, conjugation, and sentence structure are recommended but not required for non-Shakespearean speakers. Hindi and Urdu are almost 100% identical except for the alphabet. Urdu is written in the Persian alphabet and Hindi is written is Sanskrit. Grammar, accent, pronunciation, and sentence structure are recommended but not required.

Urdu

The language of Pakistan is called Urdu, and it is spoken in various other nations surrounding the Middle East. The language is taught in Pakistani school systems and by nearly all of the people of Pakistan, making it a most-learn language of the area. The language is also spoken by many people outside of the Middle East, including areas like the United States, United Kingdom, Australia, Canada and Norway. Though the main official language of India is Hindi, Urdu is still regarded as a respectable language, and many people speak both.

Spoken in: Pakistan, India, Nepal, Kashmir, and Bangladesh

I	Main
Me	Main
My	Mera
Mine	Mera
His	Iska
Him	Ye
Her	Wou
Hers	Larki
He	Larka
She	Larki
Us	Humara
Our	Tum
With you	Tumhane saath
With You {Plural}	Ugke saath
With her	Ugke saath
With him	Inke saath
With Them	Inke saath
Without me	Mere Bina
Without	Bina
Without you	Tumare Bina
Without you {Plural}	Tumare Bina
Them, They	Ye'n
Their	Inka
You	Tum
You {Plural}	Tum
I am	Main hoon
I was	Main tha
I will	Karunga
Are you	Tum kia
We	Hum
Without her	Uske Bina
Without Them	Inke Bina
Without Him	Iske Bina
With me	Mere Saath
For you	Tumare Lye
To be	Honewala
Yours	Tumahara
We are	Hum Hain
With us	Humare Saath
Without us	Humare Bina
Who	Kaun

What	Kia	**Something**	Kuch
If	Agar	**Sometimes**	Kabhi kabhi
Similar	Milta	**Somewhere**	Kahin
Where	Kahaan	**Yes**	Haan
Were	Hum	**No**	Nahi
When	Kab	**Less**	Kaam
Only	Sirf	**Instead**	Bajai
Was	Tha	**Including**	Sab milake
Other	Aur	**While**	Us doran
Since	Smce	**Someone**	Koi
Same	Ek jaisa	**Again**	Wapis
With	Is	**Away**	Janaa
Already	Phele se	**But**	Kiu
Together	Saath	**Don't**	Nahi
Then	Pher	**Both**	Dono
Than	Phir	**Because**	Isle
More	Aur	**Still, Yet**	Abhi tak
Very	Bohut	**Time**	Waat
Much, a lot	Bohut	**Time**	Us waat
From	Jagaa	**Time**	Waat
And	Aur	**Also, Too**	Phir bhi
Before	Pehle	**Around**	Charo tarat
After	Bad	**Never**	Kabhi nahi
Afterwards	Bad main	**Of course**	Zahiri baat hai
To		**Here**	Idher
The		**This**	Yeh
That	Yeh	**OK**	Ok, theek hai
That		**Just**	Bus
Is		**Although**	
Which	Kaun sa	**Through**	Paas
For		**It is**	Hai
Of		**Everywhere**	Her Jagaa
Against	Khilaf	**Ready**	Taryar
Always	Hamesha	**Soon**	Jald
Until	Tab tak	**Except**	Manzoor
Everything	Sab kuch	**Between**	Dermiyan
Every	Her ek	**Now**	Abhi
Even If	Agar phir	**Later**	Bad main
Things	Cheez	**Toward**	Samne
There	Udhar	**How Much & How Many**	Kitne kaa, kitna our
Into		**Neither**	
Or	Or	**None**	Kuch nahi
On	Upar	**Nobody**	Koi nahi
About		**Maybe**	Shyed
How	Kaisa	**Way**	Raasta
In	Under	**Why**	Kiyu
Nothing	Kuch nahi	**Side**	Side
At		**Everybody**	Her Koi
Almost	Almost	**A Few**	kuch

Small	Chotta	**Name**	Nam
Big	Bara	**Last name**	Sir name
Hot	Garam	**What is your name**	Kia naam hai tumhara
Cold	Tanda	**How old are you**	Kitne saal kai ho
Up	Upar	**Welcome**	Asalam Alikum
Down	Neeche	**Years**	Saal
Person	Insaan	**Sky**	Asmaan
People	Log	**Night**	Raath
Fast	Tez	**Light**	Roshni
Slow	Halka	**Darkness**	Andhera
Day	Din	**Morning**	Subha
Tomorrow	Kaal	**House**	Gihar
Today	Aaj	**Car**	Gari
Yesterday	Kaal	**Left**	Ulta
Good	Acha	**Right**	Seedha
Bad	Bura	**Place**	Jagaa
Hello	Saalam	**Straight**	Seedha
Goodbye	Khuda hafiz	**Parents**	Ma baap
How are you	Kaisse ho	**Book**	Kitab
Nice to meet you	Milke khushi	**Problem**	Mushkil
Good Night	Sojao	**Behind**	Peeche
Good Afternoon	Acha din	**Front**	Age
Good Morning	Acha din	**Near**	Kareeb
Friend	Dost	**Far**	Dur
Mom	Ma	**Sun**	Sooraj
Dad	Baap	**Better**	Behtar
Brother	Bhai	**Worse**	Batar
Sister	Behen	**Beautiful**	Khobsurat
Cousin	Rishtedar	**Real**	Asli
Grandfather	Dada	**Easy**	Ahsaan
Grandmother	Dadi	**Hard**	Mushkil
Please	Please	**Next**	Agla
Thank you	Shukriya	**One**	Ek
Sorry	Maafi	**Two**	Do
New	Nayi	**Three**	Teen
Inside	Under	**Four**	Char
Outside	Bahar	**Five**	Panch
Different	Hatke	**Six**	Chey
First	Pehla	**Seven**	Saat
Last	Akhri	**Eight**	Aant
Child	Bacha	**Nine**	Nau
Man	Mard	**Ten**	Dus
Women	Aurat	**Number**	Ginty
Week	Hafta	**Month**	Mahina

To Talk	Bolo na	**To Drive**	Chalana
To Walk	Chalaa	**To Pay**	Pagar dena
To Run	Bhago na	**To Buy**	Karidna
To Sleep	So na	**To Practice**	Practice kama
To Begin	Shuru karo	**To Prepare**	Teryari karna
To Finish	Khatam karo	**To Meet**	Milna
To Drink	Piyo na	**To Fly**	Urna
To Smoke	Piyo na	**To Visit**	Milna
To Prefer		**To Swim**	Terna
To Loose	Dheela rathna	**To Show**	Dikhana
To Forget	Bhulnana	**To Know**	Janaa
To Hold	Pakarna	**To Think**	Sochna
To Follow	Peecha karna	**To Believe**	Yakeen karna
To Continue	Begam na	**To Love**	Pyar karna
To Want	Chaye na	**To Like**	Pasand karna
To Stay	Rukgana	**To Use**	Istimal karna
To Keep	Pakro na	**To Try**	Koshish karna
To Play	Khelo	**To Understand**	Samaj na
To Get	Lena	**To Have**	Panaa
To Help	Madat karna	**To Happen**	Hone walaa
To Go	Chale jana	**To Recognize**	Phchchanaa
To Give	Dedena	**To Hear**	Suna
To Receive	Mangliena	**To Listen**	Suna
To Bring	Lana	**To Press**	Dabanaa
To Work	Kamkarna	**To Promise**	Wada karna
To Hope	Dua	**To Choose**	Pasand karna
To Live	Jheena	**To Arrive**	Poch jana
To Find	Dhundna	**To Leave**	Chale jana
To Look	Dhekna	**To Leave {Something}**	Chale jana
To Search	Dhunduna	**To Do**	Karna
To See	Dhekna	**To Order**	Hukum chalana
To Read	Parna	**To Pretend**	
To Write	Likhna	**To Change**	Badal na
To Learn	Seekna	**I Can**	Main karu
To Teach	Sikhana	**To Return**	Lotna
To Take	Lena	**To Borrow**	Udhar
To Turn on	Jhalana	**To Sit**	Bhetna
To Turn off	Bhuiana	**To Need**	Zaroorat
To Close	Bandkarna	**To Say**	Utha na
To Put	Rakhna	**To Remove**	Hatha dena
To Allow	Ijezat dena	**To Travel**	Safar karna
To Lift	Utha lena	**To Eat**	Khana
To Open	Chol na	**To Exchange**	Badal na
To Wish	Dua karna	**To Mix**	Milana
To Enter	Gihusna	**To Belong**	
To Come	Ajana	**To Feel**	Mehsoos kama
To Move	Hilna	**To Stop**	Rukh na
To Rent	Kiraya	**To Ask**	Puch na
To Remember	Yaad rakna	**To Answer**	Jawab dena
To Check	Check karna	**To Decide**	Te karna
To Call	Bulana	**To Sell**	Bech na
To Resemble	Milana	**To Wait**	Intizar karna

Building Bridges:

I Can	Maji karu hai
I Do	Maji Karna hai
I Go	Maji Chale jana
I Need	Maji Zaroorat
I Want	Maji Chaye na
I See	Maji Shekna hai
I Like	Maji Pasand karna bola
I Say	Maji Utha na
I Talk	Maji Bolo na

Phrases:

I do not speak Urdu

May {I} Urdu {Urdu} nahee {no} boltha {speak}

My name is

Mera {my} naam {name}.... hay {is}

Where is Bombay?

Mumbai {Bombay) kahaan {where}

Urdu is a good language

Urdu {Urdu} ayk {is} acha {good} zabaan {Language}

For the Urdu language; grammar, pronunciation, accent, conjugation, and sentence structure are recommended but not required for non-Shakespearean speakers. Urdu and Hindi are almost 100% identical except for the alphabet. Urdu is written in the Persian alphabet and Hindi is written is Sanskrit. Grammar, accent, pronunciation, and sentence structure are recommended but not required.

Asian Languages

Section IV: Malay Polynesian Languages
- Indonesian

Indonesian

Indonesian, the official language of Indonesia, stemmed from the Malay language. The primary difference is that Indonesian has more Dutch influence, though the two languages are similar when spoken. Malay is spoken in the rural parts of Indonesia, while Indonesian is spoken in the more modern and urban areas. Indonesian is actually a known dialect of Malay. Indonesians don't actually call their language Indonesian, rather, they call it Bahasa Indonesia, which translates to "Language of Indonesia."

Spoken in: Indonesia, East Timor

I	Saya
Me	Saya
My	Saya punya
Mine	Saya punya
His	Dia punya
Him	Dia
Her	Dia
Hers	Dia punya
He	Dia
She	Dia
Us	Kita
Our	Kita
With you	Sama kamu
With You {Plural}	Sama kamu
With her	Sama dia
With him	Sama dia
With Them	Sama mareka
Without me	Tampa saya
Without	Tampa
Without you	Tampa kamu
Without you {Plural}	Tampa kamu
Them, They	Mareka
Their	Mareka punya
You	Kamu, anda
You {Plural}	Kamu, anda
I am	Saya
I was	
I will	
Are you	Kamu disini
We	Kita
Without her	Tampa dia
Without Them	Tampa mareka
Without Him	Tampa dia
With me	Sama saya
For you	Buat kamu
To be	Maudisini
Yours	Kamu punya
We are	Kita orang
With us	Sama kita
Without us	Tampa kita
Who	Siaypa

What	Apa	**Something**	Sasuatu
If	Kalau	**Sometimes**	Kadang kadang
Similar	Apirsama	**Somewhere**	Sasu tampat
Where	Dimana	**Yes**	La
Were		**No**	Tida
When	Kapan	**Less**	Kurang
Only	Chuma	**Instead**	
Was		**Including**	Termosuk
Other	Lain dari	**While**	Sementara
Since	Samanyak	**Someone**	Seseorang
Same	Sama	**Again**	Lagi
With	Sama	**Away**	Jauh
Already	Sudah	**But**	Tetapi
Together	Sama sama	**Don't**	Jangan
Then	Lantas	**Both**	Bedua
Than		**Because**	Karna
More	Labih	**Still, Yet**	Masih
Very	Sangat	**Time**	Berapakali
Much, a lot	Banyak	**Time**	Waktu
From	Dari	**Time**	Jam
And	Dan	**Also, Too**	Juga
Before	Sebulumya	**Around**	Kaliling
After	Sesudanyah	**Never**	Tidakaparnah
Afterwards	Sesudanyah	**Of course**	Tantusaja
To	Ke	**Here**	Sine
The		**This**	Ini
That	Ini	**OK**	Ok
That		**Just**	Barusan
Is		**Although**	Walaupun
Which	Yangmana	**Through**	Lawat
For	Buat	**It is**	Ini
Of		**Everywhere**	Dimasaja
Against		**Ready**	Salasai
Always	Salalu	**Soon**	Sepatnya
Until	Sampai	**Except**	Salain
Everything	Samura	**Between**	Antara
Every	Samua	**Now**	Sekarang
Even If	Walaupun	**Later**	Nanti
Things	Barng	**Toward**	Ke
There	Sana	**How Much & How Many**	Barapa banyak
Into	Masuk	**Neither**	
Or	Atau	**None**	Tidakada
On	Atas	**Nobody**	Tida kada orang
About		**Maybe**	Mung kin
How	Bagaimana	**Way**	Jalan mana
In	Dalam	**Why**	Kena pa
Nothing	Tidak ada	**Side**	Samping
At	Di	**Everybody**	Samua orang
Almost	Hampir	**A Few**	Beberapa

Small	Kecil	**Name**	Nama
Big	Besar	**Last name**	Nama keluarga
Hot	Panas	**What is your name**	Apa nama mu
Cold	Dingin	**How old are you**	Umurberapa
Up	Atas	**Welcome**	Salamak
Down	Bawa	**Years**	Tahun
Person	Orang	**Sky**	Langit
People	Orang	**Night**	Malam
Fast	Cepat	**Light**	Lampu
Slow	Lambat	**Darkness**	Malamgalap
Day	Hari	**Morning**	Pagi
Tomorrow	Basok	**House**	Rumah
Today	Jari ini	**Car**	Mobile
Yesterday	Kemarin	**Left**	Kiri
Good	Bagus	**Right**	Kanan
Bad	Jahat	**Place**	Tempat
Hello	Hello	**Straight**	Taruz
Goodbye	Bye, da	**Parents**	Orangtua
How are you	Apakabar	**Book**	Buku
Nice to meet you		**Problem**	Persoalan
Good Night	Salamat idur	**Behind**	Belakang
Good Afternoon	Salamat siang	**Front**	Depan
Good Morning	Salamat pagi	**Near**	Dekat
Friend	Sehabat	**Far**	Jauh
Mom	Ebuk	**Sun**	Matahari
Dad	Ajah	**Better**	Lebihbagus
Brother	Saudaralaki	**Worse**	Lebihjalak
Sister	Saudaraprenpuan	**Beautiful**	Bagus
Cousin	Sepupu	**Real**	Benar
Grandfather	Kakek	**Easy**	Gampag
Grandmother	Kenek	**Hard**	Sulit
Please	Selahkan	**Next**	
Thank you	Terimakasih	**One**	Sutu
Sorry	Maaf	**Two**	Dua
New	Baru	**Three**	Tiga
Inside	Dalam	**Four**	Ampat
Outside	Diluar	**Five**	Lima
Different	Lain	**Six**	Anam
First	Pertama	**Seven**	Tujuh
Last	Terahir	**Eight**	Delapan
Child	Anak	**Nine**	Sembilian
Man	Lelkli	**Ten**	Sepuluh
Women	Wonita	**Number**	Nomer
Week	Mingu	**Month**	Bulan

To Talk	Bechara	**To Drive**	Setir
To Walk	Jalan	**To Pay**	Bayar
To Run	Berlari	**To Buy**	Belile
To Sleep	Tidur	**To Practice**	Practak
To Begin	Mulai	**To Prepare**	Setiakan
To Finish	Habisin	**To Meet**	Ketemu
To Drink	Minum	**To Fly**	Terbag
To Smoke	Isap	**To Visit**	Bertemu
To Prefer	Lebihsuka	**To Swim**	Berenag
To Loose		**To Show**	Lihatin
To Forget	Lupa	**To Know**	Tahu
To Hold	Pagang	**To Think**	Pikir
To Follow	Berikut	**To Believe**	Perchaya
To Continue	Turuskan	**To Love**	Chinta
To Want	Mau	**To Like**	Suka
To Stay	Tingal	**To Use**	Pakai
To Keep	Seimpan	**To Try**	Choba
To Play	Bermain	**To Understand**	Mengerti
To Get	Ambil	**To Have**	Kepunyan
To Help	Bantu	**To Happen**	Terjadi
To Go	Bergi	**To Recognize**	Inget
To Give	Kasih	**To Hear**	Dengar
To Receive	Terima	**To Listen**	Dengar
To Bring	Bawak	**To Press**	Tekan
To Work	Kerja	**To Promise**	Janji
To Hope	Harapan	**To Choose**	Pilih
To Live	Hidup	**To Arrive**	Jampai
To Find	Dapat	**To Leave**	Pergi
To Look	Lihat	**To Leave {Something}**	Tingalin
To Search	Selikdik	**To Do**	Kerji
To See	Lihat	**To Order**	Pesan
To Read	Bacha	**To Pretend**	Purak purak
To Write	Menulis	**To Change**	Berganti
To Learn	Belajar	**I Can**	Saya bisa
To Teach	Menajar	**To Return**	Kembali
To Take	Menganbil	**To Borrow**	Pinjam
To Turn on	Pesang	**To Sit**	Buduk
To Turn off	Matikan	**To Need**	Perlu
To Close	Tutup	**To Say**	Bilng
To Put	Turuh	**To Remove**	Pindahin
To Allow	Bolehkan	**To Travel**	
To Lift	Angkat	**To Eat**	Makan
To Open	Buka	**To Exchange**	Berganti
To Wish	Permintakan	**To Mix**	Champur kan
To Enter	Musuk	**To Belong**	Kepunyann
To Come	Datang	**To Feel**	Merasa
To Move	Pindah	**To Stop**	Berhentikan
To Rent	Sawa	**To Ask**	Pertanyaan
To Remember	Ingat	**To Answer**	Jawapan
To Check	Lihat	**To Decide**	Pilih
To Call	Pangil	**To Sell**	Jual
To Resemble	Mirip	**To Wait**	Tungu

Building Bridges

I Can	Saya bisa
I Do	Saya Kerji
I Go	Saya Bergi
I Need	Saya Perlu
I Want	Saya Mau
I See	Saya Lihat
I Like	Saya Suka
I Say	Saya Bilng
I Talk	Saya Bechara

Phrases:

My name is Michael
Nama saya Michael
Nama {name} saya {my} Michael

You don't understand
Anda tidak mengerti
Anda {you} tidak {no} mengerti {understand}

I'm sorry, I do not speak the Indonesian language
Maaf, saya tidak dapat Bechara Bahasa Indonesia
Maaf {sorry}, saya {I} tidak {no} dapat Bechara {speak}
Bahasa {the language} Indonesia

For the Indonesian language; grammar, pronunciation, accent, conjugation, reading, and sentence structure are recommended but not required for non-Shakespearean speakers.

Note to the Reader

If you merely absorb the required 350 words, in any of the 27 languages in this book, you will then have acquired the most comprehensive ultimate foundational basis that was ever created to become conversational in a foreign language!! After choosing the language of your desire and memorizing these 350 words, then, this "conversational foundational basis" that you have just gained will trigger your ability to make improvements in conversational fluency at the rate of the speed of light! However, in order to engage in fluent communication you need a special type of basics, and this book will provide you with just that, guaranteed.

Unlike the current foreign language learning systems presently used in schools and universities, along with books and programs that are available on the market today, that all focus on EVERYTHING but being conversational, by contrast, THIS method's sole focus is on becoming conversational. Once you have successfully mastered the required words in this book, in the language of your choice, there are two techniques that, if combined with these essential words, can further enhance your skills and will result in you improving your fluency tenfold. HOWEVER THOSE TWO TECHNIQUES WILL ONLY SUCCEED IF you have completely and successfully absorbed the 350 words.

The first step is to attend a language class that will enable you to sharpen your grammar. You will gain additional vocabulary, learn past and present tenses and if you apply these skills which you learn in the class, together with the 350 words that you have previously memorized, you will be improving your conversational skills ten fold. You will notice that "conversational wise" you will succeed at a much higher rate than any of your other classmates. A simple second technique is to choose foreign language subtitles, in that language, while watching a movie. If you have successfully mastered and grasped these 350 words, then the combination of the two, those words along with the subtitles, will aid you considerably in putting all the grammar into prospective, and again conversational wise you will improve ten fold.

Once you have established a basis of fluent conversation, resulting from those words which you just attained, then every additional word or grammar rule you pick up from there on, can be combined with them (the 350 words) enriching.your conversational abilities even more. Basically after the research and studies I conducted with my method over the years, I came to the conclusion that in order to become conversational you must first must learn the words AND then learn the grammar.

Several of the languages in this book are also compatible with the mirror translation technique. Likewise with THOSE languages, you can use this mirror translation technique in order to become conversational, enabling one to communicate even more fluently. Mirror translation is the method of translating a phrase or sentence, word per word from English to another language, by using these imperative words which you have acquired through this program. Latin languages, Middle Eastern languages, Slavic languages along with a few others are also compatible with the mirror translation technique. Though you won't be speaking Shakespearean, you will still be fully understood and conversation-wise, able to get by just fine.

For example in Spanish, a language which is compatible with mirror translation, if we say *"The house that I like is very small"* la(the) casa(house) que(that) me(I) gusta(like) es(is) muy(very) pequeño(small). However the Chinese language is not compatible with mirror translation, *"The house which I like is very small"*, will be wo(I) xi-huan(like) de(of) fang-zi(house) tai(very) xiao(small) [In Chinese the article *is* doesn't exist]. So please do not attempt the mirror translation technique with Chinese.

Conclusion

You now have the tools to master 27 languages. I hope that this has been a valuable experience, and that you have successful communications across the globe in whatever journeys you endeavor. Not to mention the many other things this book is useful for. I hope this book will connect people from all corners of the globe from all cultures and religions together, hopefully for the good.

After you choose a language of your desire in this book and memorized the 5 pages, then congratulations you now know a language. Whether that be to impress your friends, get a language under your belt, or be able to put a language on your resume. By memorizing the 5 pages of the language of your desire you have now completed most of the puzzle and can see the 'big picture' in terms of how to communicate the language. Now you have an EXCELLENT basis in order to expand on the language and go farther to master the final pieces of the puzzle if desired.

6083422R00122

Printed in Germany
by Amazon Distribution
GmbH, Leipzig